THE OPTION OF URBANISM

CHRISTOPHER B. LEINBERGER

THE OPTION OF URBANISM

Investing in a New American Dream

ISLANDPRESS

Washington ▪ Covelo ▪ London

Published by Island Press

Library of Congress Cataloging-in-Publication Data

Leinberger, Christopher B.
   The option of urbanism : investing in a new American dream / by Christopher B. Leinberger.
      p. cm.
   Includes bibliographical references and index.
   ISBN-13: 978-1-59726-136-4 (hardcover : alk. paper)
   ISBN-13: 978-1-59726-137-1 (pbk. : alk. paper)
   1. Urbanization—United States.   2. Community development, Urban.   3. Suburbs—United States.   4. Cities and towns—Growth—United States.   5. City planning—United States.   6. Sustainable development—United States.   I. Title.
   HT384.U5L45 2008
   307.760973—dc22   2007026186

Printed on recycled, acid-free paper ✺

Manufactured in the United States of America
10   9   8   7   6   5   4   3   2   1

Search terms: urban, suburban, sprawl, auto-dependent, real estate product development types, transportation, Futurama, affordable housing, inclusionary zoning, impact fees, New Urbanism, transit-oriented development, American Dream, S&L crisis, walkable urbanism, drivable sub-urbanism, global warming, carbon load, obesity, asthma, favored quarter, metropolitan, regionalism, urbanization, population growth, REIT

For Helen, Lisa, and Tom

Also for Bob, Gadi, Joe, Pat, and Robert

CONTENTS

PREFACE TO THE
PAPERBACK EDITION

In the nearly two years since this book was written, much has changed in the built environment —real estate and infrastructure—and the economy. Once again, the way in which we have invested in the built environment, which is quantified in this book as thirty-five percent of the financial assets of the American economy, has led the way to a major economic recession. Two of the past three economic recessions—that of the early 1990s and the current one, which started in early 2008—were caused by real estate overbuilding and careless real estate financing. The third recession, caused by the high-tech bust of the early 2000s, saw the Federal Reserve use real estate as an effective counterforce, making that downturn far less severe but setting up the current recession to be much worse.

The current recession is quite significant, and not only for its severity and probable long length. It is significant because it has been primarily, though not exclusively, caused by the *structural* change in how America builds itself. We are not experiencing a *cyclical* downturn. The current economic downturn is being caused by a fundamental shift in how America invests the thrity-five percent of our assets that constitutes the built environment. This shift cannot help but have an impact on the economy. As evidence, we see strong signs that the bulk of the decline in housing values has affected the kind of housing that this book refers to as *drivable sub-urban*, which has been substantially overbuilt. In contrast, the type of housing that this book refers to as *walkable urban*—where most everyday needs can be met by walking or by transit—has largely held its value. As a result, there is vast overbuilding and abandonment of one type of development while there is pent-up demand for the other type of development.

Oversupply of inventory is the primary cause of an economic slow-down. This can be caused by a reduction in production (and therefore employment) in hopes of either waiting for the existing demand to consume any excess inventory or waiting for overextended consumers and businesses to correct their personal or corporate balance sheets. Consumer confidence also plays a major role in the creation of oversupply, especially when consumers consider real estate, since it is such a large capital commitment that most people and companies only make when they have confidence in their future earnings potential.

This recession is caused both by an oversupply of primarily drivable sub-urban residential real estate (there has also been oversupply of walkable urban condominiums in select markets) and by overextended consumers. This recession has been compounded by overly complex financial mortgage instruments (securitization), which hid problem loans and spread them around the globe. Adding to the severity of the situation, for many of the drivable sub-urban houses behind these mortgages, the house will likely never be worth anything close to the face value of its mortgage, much less the replacement value of its construction. If these underlying assets become slums—defined as areas where market value is worth much less than replacement value, thus providing no economic incentive to maintain properties—the mortgages become what has come to be called *toxic*.

The fundamental change in how we invest the American Dream on the ground was accelerated by a series of ideological decisions by Bush administration officials to not regulate real estate–oriented and other financial instruments. The ideological culprits in this recession are many, and include:

- the Security and Exchange Commission's decision to deregulate investment banks, especially regarding real estate securitization;

- Fannie Mae and Freddie Mac's decision to finance subprime mort-gage–backed securities as part of the *ownership society*;
- the decision by Chairman of the Federal Reserve Alan Greenspan to not regulate mortgage brokers, thinking the invisible hand of the market would suffice—a mistake he has since acknowledged;
- the Bush administration's Treasury Department decision to not regulate credit swaps, the primary cause of the bankruptcy and nationalization of AIG, the largest insurance company in the world;
- credit-rating agencies engaged in underwriting of mortgages and other assets they had no experience with, violating long-established practice;
- investment bankers' bonuses, driven by short-term earnings, regardless of long-term risk;
- the crash of the car industry, partially due to the market's rejection of its cars and consumer financing difficulties, but also to the fact that vehicle miles driven peaked in 2004, according to a 2008 Brookings Institution study,[1] and are beginning to decline, possibly because of the shift to walkable urbanism; and
- households in debt because of car loans, education loans, and credit cards.

All of this led to the freezing of the banking system for an economy addicted to debt.

However, when economists write the history of this recession, it will be the structural shift in how we invest in the built environment—how the American Dream is laid out on the ground—that will stand out as the root cause.

There have been constant parallels drawn between this recession and the Great Depression of the 1930s, many of which are apt. However, another meaningful comparison is between the current shift in how we

---

[1]Puentes, R. and A. Tomer, "The Road . . . Less Traveled: An Analysis of Vehicle Miles Traveled Trends in the U.S.," The Brookings Institution, December 16, 2008.

build the built environment and the last shift which occurred during the post–World War II years of the 1940s and 1950s.

It was in the postwar years that the American households living in city centers began to leave for the suburbs, switching from living in walkable urbanism to drivable sub-urbanism. This era also coincided with the boom in the economy driven by car manufacturing, maintenance, financing, and road building. As a result, cities that were comprised of middle and upper-middle class families in the early twentieth century were abandoned to low-income households. Urban homes lost so much value that it did not make sense for the new occupants to invest in them. If a new dollar of investment in a home cannot be recouped upon resale, there is no financial motivation to invest. This resulted in the transformation of initially well-built and maintained homes into the huge urban slums of the 1960s and subsequent decades.

The majority of cities in this country became uninhabitable for anyone who had a choice following the Second World War. The white picket fence, lawn, and two-car garage available in the predominantly drivable suburbs became the very expression of who we were as a people, the definition of the American Dream. It became what we wanted, what we subsidized, what we made legal to build, what we knew how to finance and build, and what we bought. Most of our grandparents or parents wanted it, as do many, though by no means all, contemporary American households.

The pent-up demand for the drivable sub-urban American Dream took fifty years to satisfy. Every time the economy was driven into recession—most times by the real estate industry—inventories of unsold homes or unrented office, apartment or industrial space grew. However, these cyclical recessions were always cured by time, two to three years at most. The recessionary inventory imbalance of too much drivable sub-urban product was always corrected in the first few years of a recovery.

Unfortunately, time will probably not cure today's huge overhang of real estate, which is supported by the huge investment in infrastructure we have made. The vast majority of the real estate problem in the current recession is located on the far fringes of our metropolitan areas and is composed predominately of drivable sub-urban housing and commercial space. There is an exception to this situation, caused by the overbuilding of high-density condominiums in many city centers, especially Miami and Las Vegas. Some condominiums are in walkable urban settings, though many are not. These projects will find a market given time, because the market ultimately wants them, but the sub-urban real estate will go unpurchased.

In March of 2008, I wrote an article for *The Atlantic* entitled "The Next Slum?" It pointed out that because of this structural change in how we define the American Dream—from drivable sub-urban to walkable urban—we are shifting our slums to the fringe of our metropolitan areas, car-dependent places and, many times, in neighborhoods that have been recently built. It was one of the ten most downloaded stories of 2008 for the magazine. Subsequent to that article's appearance, most major news outlets (*New York Times, Time, The Economist, Newsweek, Business Week,* etc.), have run major stories about this trend. The very drivable sub-urban homes and commercial developments that were built in the 1990s and 2000s are most likely to be where new slums will develop. The price declines on the fringes of drivable sub-urban places have been so severe that it makes no financial sense to invest that next dollar in a home—the definition of a slum as introduced above.

A new Web site, http://www.WalkScore.com, was unveiled since this book was originally published. It allows every homeowner in the country to enter their home address and quickly determine how walkable or drivable their house is using a scale of zero to one hundred. A Walk Score of zero to thirty is considered *extremely drivable*—virtually every trip by home requires a car, including trips to school, coffee shops, grocery stores, or work. Without automobile or bus transportation, people in such areas cannot fully participate in many societal activities. A Walk Score of seventy to one hundred means that most daily needs are located within walking distance from people's homes.

Preliminary findings from this national database appear to show that there are significant price differences between drivable sub-urban housing and walkable urban housing—walkable urban housing is much more valuable. Twenty to thirty years ago, the largest housing for the *cheapest* price, i.e., the lowest price per square foot, could be found in walkable urban neighborhoods, often in the slums of the day. Today, walkable urban neighborhoods are often the most valuable in many metropolitan areas and have largely held their value during this crushing housing depression.

The run-up in oil prices in 2008 showed that American households are very sensitive to high oil prices and accelerated the trend toward walkable urban development; but it did not cause it. The long-term exhaustion of fossil fuels and the need to address climate change, both of which will increase oil prices, will add further impetus to the market trend toward walkable urban development.

The structural shift in how we build the built environment, the shift from drivable sub-urban to walkable urban, was the catalyst for the current recession and is the reason why it will probably be such a long downturn. It will take time for the research findings to be gathered; but if the recently developed drivable sub-urban housing on the fringe turns into the next slums, the real estate boom of the 1990s and this decade will become known as the last gasp of sprawl.

This is not to say that *all* drivable sub-urban development has gone out of favor. Many households and businesses prefer this low-density development pattern, and they should certainly be allowed to have it. There is simply too much product on the market. In addition, drivable suburbia continues to be subsidized. While we should celebrate choice, one choice should not be subsidized over the other.

The issue is that today, and for the next generation, there is and will continue to be huge pent-up demand for the alternative—higher-density, walkable urban development. This is similar to the pent-up demand for drivable sub-urban development in the postwar period that took decades to satisfy. The problem is that the public policy makers in the U.S. do not yet understand this. As this is being written, the new Obama administration continues to talk about the need to stimulate the economy through the building of "roads and bridges." If this continues to be the domestic policy of the country, we will be using the strategy of the last war to fight the next one. Only through investment in infrastructure appropriate for walkable urban development can we begin to dig the economy out of the ditch it is in. As this book explains, *transportation drives development.* The transportation system our society chooses to invest in will dictate the form of the built environment.

There is a crucial need to build out the second half of the American transportation system—rail transit, bicycle and pedestrian—while maintaining the existing highway system that is in such a sorry state of repair. There is a need to invest in high-speed rail to link major metropolitan areas, create gateway ports, reinvent the airline system, and rebuild the barge and freight-railway systems. All of these great efforts need to be networked to one another to maximize efficiencies.

This investment will be expensive and will not be achieved by public dollars alone. The requirements far exceed the available public resources. However, the public dollars must lead and show the way to the twenty first-century transportation system we desperately need. America is being lapped by Europe, Japan, Korea, and China. So, so there is little time to lose.

The private sector must be open to sharing the financial benefits of improved and enhanced transportation infrastructure through what is referred to as *value capture*, the long-held idea that private interests should share the financial upside created by public investment by helping to pay for those public investments. Encouraging future private property value increases to help pay for the transportation improvements that caused those value increases is needed if the huge price tag required is to be paid. In exchange, the federal government must establish an infrastructure bank to help provide credit enhancement needed to unlock this future value.

The next step is to ensure that appropriate, high-density zoning is established around existing and new rail transit stations to take advantage of the demand for walkable urban development. Existing zoning regulations and the not-in-my-backyard (NIMBY) sentiment are major obstacles in the way of creating higher densities and meeting this demand. The primary way to overcome the NIMBY opposition to walkable urbanism is by bringing the surrounding neighborhoods into the planning process. It is time to stop asking the private real estate development community to plan our future. Community members need to engage in the multiyear process needed to determine how they want to grow in the future, recognizing that "no growth" is not an option.

In addition, organizations need to be established to develop the strategy and provide the management of these walkable urban places. These places are vastly more complicated to build and maintain than conventional drivable sub-urban places, and they need full-time management.

A final major issue that needs immediate attention is the unintended consequences caused by the pent-up demand for walkable urban development—gentrification and the need for affordable and workforce housing. There is a need for conscious strategies to insure *mixed-income,* as well as *mixed-use*, walkable urban places.

The next American Dream is an exciting prospect for this country, providing a choice of either drivable sub-urban or walkable urban development, depending on taste, lifestyle, and time of life. Significantly, the walkable urban alternative is far more energy efficient and environmentally sustainable. It builds household wealth faster, reduces many of the now-chronic health conditions that bedevil modern society (obesity, diabetes, asthma, etc.), and builds a greater sense of community. All of these issues are addressed in this book.

And the redeployment of thirty-five percent of the assets in the American economy toward a walkable urban built environment is a major way in which we can pull ourselves out of the current steep recession and power the economy for many decades. Real estate and infrastructure investment has always been a way to spark economic recovery in our country, and the demand for walkable urban development will prove to be a major engine of economic growth for the next generation. Let's get to work.

PREFACE TO THE HARDCOVER EDITION

When I was a young child my mother took me to Center City, Philadelphia from our inner-suburban home to visit my father in his office and to go shopping. This was in the mid-1950s, so Center City was still the vibrant center of the entire metropolitan area. My mother and I walked three blocks from our single-family home three blocks to a trolley stop that took us to the terminus of the subway that in turn took us to Center City. This day trip was obviously memorable; even a half century later.

After visiting my father, we went to the grand retail emporium, John Wanamaker's, which was on Market Street. It was one of the greatest department store buildings in the country and included the locally well-known twenty-foot-high, 2,500-pound bronze sculpture of an eagle in the center of the four-story central courtyard, flanked by the largest musical instrument in the world, the Wanamaker organ, with pipes that rose three floors. The building maintains its beauty and grandeur to this day, now a Macy's department store.

However, what made the biggest impact on me that day was walking toward Wanamaker's on Market Street. I firmly gripped my mother's hand, looking up at her from my two-foot height disadvantage. I was completely hemmed in by more people than I had ever been around in my short life. In my mind's eye, I floated up a few hundred feet and looked down on where my mother and I were. I saw this crush of people, all rushing somewhere. However, on the side streets off Market, there seemed to be very few people on the sidewalks. I wondered, "Why are there so many people here and not elsewhere?" Little did I realize then, but that was the question I would seek to answer for the bulk of my career. It is the basis of how we structure the built environment and real estate economics.

The inner-suburban neighborhood where we lived was built in the 1920s, a time during which many observers feel that the best suburbs ever created were built—a precursor to what is referred to as New Urbanism today. The area had everything a youngster needed within walking or bicycling distance. The local drug, variety, and grocery stores were three blocks away, and the local "downtown," with a movie theater, A&P "super market," post office, and midrise apartment buildings, was eight blocks away. Elementary, junior high, and senior high schools were all within walking distance, which resulted in my walking an estimated 2,200 miles over my twelve-year public school career.

Fast forward. When I was a teenager in the mid-1960s, living in the same inner-suburban home and neighborhood, my mother took me on another shopping trip, this time to the newly opened King of Prussia Mall, the first regional mall in the area, at the intersection of the Pennsylvania Turnpike and the Schuylkill Expressway. The mall was in the opposite direction from Center City and accessible only by car. When we arrived, I thought I had died and gone to heaven; I was enamored with all the stores clustered in one place. We got there by driving on the expressway, getting on at City Line Avenue using soaring on-ramps, the first major interchange in the region. I was equally enamored with these ramps and the expressway, thinking that someday Philadelphia would become a *big city,* just like Los Angeles. Many times on television I had seen the four-level freeway interchange in downtown LA and hoped that was the future we were heading toward.

I was not alone in my adoration of what was a new and entirely different way of building our metropolitan areas. I was just part of the country's overwhelming desire and demand for what was a radical and unprecedented future. The market wanted it, and the market got it.

As an adult I have lived in a broad range of urban, suburban, and exurban locations. We first settled in cities and then in classic suburban locations when my children were born. As my children were growing, we moved to an exurban location with plenty of land, though the children's grade school and the country store and post office were all across the road within walking distance. Today, as empty-nesters, my wife and I live in a dense walkable city, able to walk or take transit to just about everything. We use the one car in the household about once a week. My family has experienced just about all forms of metropolitan living possible and has enjoyed each one.

Attempting to answer that question I first posed to myself on Market Street in Center City, Philadelphia eventually led me to my first career as a real estate consultant. As the managing director and co-owner of Robert Charles Lesser & Co., the nation's largest independent real estate advisory firm, I focused on how metropolitan areas grew, writing extensively about this topic for national magazines, academic journals, and real estate industry publications. The question also led me to assist real estate development companies in addressing these trends through their corporate strategic planning. My second career shifted me toward implementation as a real estate developer, attempting the first Western-led effort to redevelop parts of downtown St. Petersburg, Russia, in the early 1990s, helping start the redevelopment effort in downtown Albuquerque, New Mexico, in the late 1990s, and developing New Urbanist projects in the Kansas City and Philadelphia metropolitan areas in the early 2000s. Part-time graduate-level teaching and writing during both of my first two careers took me to a third career. I helped start the graduate real estate program at the University of Michigan and became a visiting fellow at The Brookings Institution in Washington, D.C.

The answer to the question of why people want to be in some locations and not in others is vitally important. It affects all aspects of our lives. But as will be shown, it has significant, though underappreciated, impact on many crucial social, economic, environmental, political, financial; and international issues facing us in the twenty-first century. It is more important than even to understand how our society continues to answer that question; we need to consider the options and very carefully make informed decisions.

Introduction

W hen I teach a graduate real estate seminar, the first home-
work I give to the students is watching the 1985 movie *Back
to the Future*. The film reflects most of the fundamental changes in how
America has been built over the past sixty years. Michael J. Fox, playing the lead character, is a teenager growing up in 1985 suburban Hill
Valley. Automobiles are nearly the only way folks get around in 1985
Hill Valley, though Michael J. Fox, riding his skateboard, would hop a
ride hanging onto the bumper of a car. The 1985 Hill Valley downtown
is where homeless people sleep, X-rated films are shown, and very little
else happens.

In the film, Michael J. Fox is transported back to 1955 to a very different Hill Valley (figure 0.1). Downtown is the center of life, with the
malt shop where the teens hang out, many movie theaters playing family
fare, shops, office workers, housing within walking distance, and mid-
dle- and working-class people on the sidewalks. The 1955 Hill Valley is
actually a reflection of the pre-World War II era, when the bulk of this
fictional downtown would have been built. Very little was built in this
country during the Depression in the 1930s, aside from federal govern-
ment-funded relief projects, or during the Second World War, aside from
military-funded development. Therefore, 1955 downtown Hill Valley is

FIGURE 0.1. The 1955 downtown Hill Valley in *Back to the Future* was the hub of the town, with people from all walks of life walking, biking, and driving to get there and generally walking among stores and offices once downtown, as Michael J. Fox is doing crossing the square. (Source: Courtesy of Universal Studios Licensing LLLP)

a reflection of typical small town life in this country during the early twentieth century.

However, a large-scale social experiment—the result of an unofficial domestic policy at the federal, state, and local levels—fundamentally transformed the country during the late twentieth century. The citizens of this country were eager and willing participants in this social experiment. This policy produced the Hill Valley of 1985 (figure 0.2)—a form of human settlement never before seen in the United States or anywhere else in the world.

The two Hill Valleys show the only two viable divergent options we have in how to build our metropolitan built environment—which consists of the houses, roads, water and sewer lines, police and fire stations, office buildings, shops, factories, parks, and everything else that makes up where most Americans live, work, and play.

Much of the debate and discussion about the built environment has been about cities versus suburbs. The fact that one of the major categorizations

FIGURE 0.2. The 1985 downtown Hill Valley was where X-rated movies were shown, few offices or stores were open, and the homeless slept. The square had become an asphalt parking lot. The hub of the town had shifted to the regional mall on the outskirts of town. (Source: Courtesy of Universal Studios Licensing LLLP)

of U.S. Census data has been the split in demographic trends between city and suburb is a primary reason for this. This book will show that there is a more pertinent way of categorizing the built environment.

The 1955 downtown Hill Valley option can be described as *walkable urbanism,* which means that you could satisfy most everyday needs, such as school, shopping, parks, friends, and even employment, within walking distance or transit of one's home. Walkable urbanism as a description combines the basic transportation mode used with the character of the place. Walking distance is generally defined as a 1,500- to 3,000-foot radius—a quarter to a half mile—which means densities must be relatively high to have all those options available so close by, hence the reference to urbanism. Trips beyond this distance generally require considering an alternative means of transportation, which throughout history have included horses, rail transit, bikes, buses, cars, and recently, Segway personal transporters. Prior to the Second World War, walkable urbanism was the primary option offered to Americans living in metropolitan areas. It was how we had been building cities since mankind started building them—that is, until the last sixty years.

THE RISE OF DRIVABLE SUB-URBANISM

How we've built for the past sixty years, the 1985 Hill Valley option, can be described as *drivable sub-urbanism*, which means that we get in our car for nearly every trip we take because the buildings are arranged in a very low density, hence the reference to sub-urban. Drivable sub-urbanism as a description, like walkable urbanism, combines the basic transportation mode used with the character of the place. There were selective examples of drivable sub-urbanism in the early part of the twentieth century prior to the building slowdown caused by the 1930s Depression and the Second World War. This was just a warm-up for the last half of the century, when drivable sub-urbanism became the basis of the American economy, the unofficial domestic policy, and the American Dream.

While drivable sub-urbanism predominantly occurs in the suburbs of a metropolitan area, there are many examples of drivable sub-urbanism in existing cities: high-income Sherman Oaks and low-income Watts, both within the City of Los Angeles, are drivable sub-urban places. Likewise, there are a number of examples of walkable urbanism in the suburbs, and probably the majority of future walkable urban places will be built in the suburbs. This is why demographic research that divides American metropolitan areas into just cities and suburbs has become less relevant of late.

Drivable sub-urban neighborhoods are built at a very low density, reflecting that automobiles and trucks are the only practical form of transportation there. This style of development has been disparagingly referred to as "sprawl," but it is obviously a market-accepted way of organizing society. In fact, today it seems like an immutable part of the American Dream. It is the way most Americans think life has to be lived, because it has been basically the only option we have been given for two generations. If we wanted to buy a new middle-class or upper-middle-class house in Atlanta or Phoenix or Columbus over the past half century, a single-family house with a yard has been about the only option. When we've gone grocery shopping, most of us have had the option of going to a 1980s strip mall or a 1990s strip mall. Take your pick. America provides choice galore once we get into the grocery store, but in recent years most of us have had only one choice in the type of environment in which we live, work, and play.

THE PENDULUM SWINGS

It's as if the built environment pendulum (figure 0.3), which was stuck on primarily building walkable urban places for thousands of years, became unstuck after the Second World War and swung all the way over to the newly available alternative—drivable sub-urbanism. It now seems like the pendulum swung too far in that direction, as would be expected, but that it is just beginning to swing back, providing a choice of both walkable urban and drivable sub-urban development for the first time.

This is in large part due to the resurgence of market demand for walkable urbanism since the early to mid-1990s. Most of the larger downtowns in the country have seen a surprising revitalization since the early 1990s, spurred by urban entertainment, followed by housing (rental and for-sale) and local-serving retail. In a couple of downtowns, new office-based jobs are now being added, reversing a sixty-year decline in regional market share. The design and planning movement known as New Urbanism, which focuses on the development of walkable urban places, generally located in the suburbs, emerged during the same time period and took the planning and development industries by storm. Started with an almost religious fervor by a group of mainly planners and architects, it has become a major force in changing zoning codes and suburban development in many U.S. states and now abroad. In addition, abandoned strip and regional malls have been transformed into high-density housing, retail, and work places, knitted together by a walkable urban street grid. Many of these new and redeveloped places, including some downtowns and downtown-adjacent places that many middle-class people would not have even

The Pendulum Moves in How America Invests 35% of Our Wealth

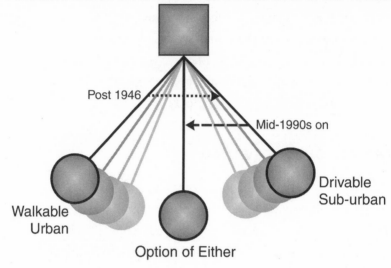

FIGURE 0.3. Movement of the pendulum between the two options of how to construct the built environment, swinging from the pre-Depression walkable urbanism to the last half of the twentieth century's drivable sub-urbanism. The pendulum is just beginning to swing back to where *both* are options.

visited on a dare fifteen to twenty years ago, have seen their rental rates and per-square-foot sales prices become the highest in their metropolitan area. I will discuss recent consumer research that shows that inhabitants of thirty to forty percent of households in the surveyed metropolitan areas want to live in walkable urban places, yet only five to twenty percent of the housing supply would be considered walkable in most regions.

In this book, I assert that this change of preference is profound, because in walkable urban places, more development leads to better communities. By adding new development to walkable urban communities they thrive—more development supports more shops, more transit, more street life, increased property values and taxes. This has not been the case with drivable sub-urban development. New drivable sub-urban housing subdivisions, strip retail, and office parks lead to more traffic, increased pollution, and less open space—and often result in great opposition to new growth. The United States faces a conundrum in how to grow *and* provide a high quality of life that is sustainable. Walkable urbanism is a crucial part of the answer.

And grow we will. The U.S. population numbered over 300 million people in 2006. Predictions show that the next 100 million people will be added in another thirty-six to forty-two years (either by 2043, according to the U.S. Census, or by 2049, according to the United Nations).[1] The United States will add that next 100 million people faster than every country on the planet, except for India and China. (Pakistan is growing at about the same rate as the United States in absolute terms).

Where do most Americans currently live, and where will the next 100 million live? In metropolitan areas. Currently, eighty-three percent of Americans live in the country's 361 metropolitan areas, as defined by the US Census.[2] Another six percent live in "exurbia"[3] outside these metropolitan areas and rely on their closest metro area for their livelihood.[4] These percentages are projected to increase, continuing a 200-year trend.

Changing the built environment is critical for many reasons, but none is more important to most people than economic growth. Economic growth is one of the primary requirements for most people's personal fulfillment, for societal and personal wealth creation, for the reduction of global tensions, and for environmental protection. It is not generally known that the built environment—the houses, office buildings, manufacturing plants, highways, transit lines, parks, government buildings, power plants, and all the infrastructure that supports them—plays a dominant role in our economy. If you just so happened to buy the United States of America, you would have to write a check for over $200 trillion. Of that amount, you would be paying about $70 trillion for the built environment, or thirty-five percent of all assets in the U.S. economy.[5] The built environment is the largest asset class in the economy, larger than all corporations traded on all the various stock exchanges, all privately owned companies, cash on hand, all public and private art collections, or any other asset class (figure 0.4). More people listed on the *Forbes 400* of the wealthiest Americans made their money in real estate than in any

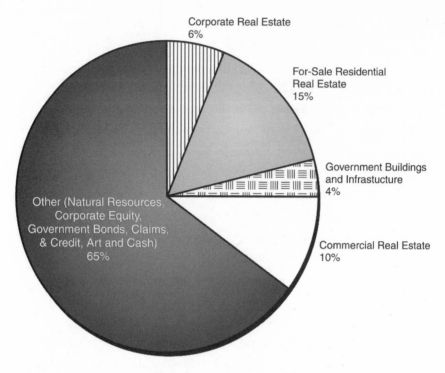

Corporate Real Estate
6%

For-Sale Residential
Real Estate
15%

Government Buildings
and Infrastucture
4%

Other (Natural Resources,
Corporate Equity,
Government Bonds, Claims,
& Credit, Art and Cash)
65%

Commercial Real Estate
10%

FIGURE 0.4. The built environment (corporate, for-sale residential, government buildings and infrastructure, and commercial real estate) represents thirty-five percent of the assets of the American economy—the largest single asset class. (Source: Roulac Global Places, LLC)

other industry. The average American household's largest financial asset is real estate.

Today we may be moving toward a virtual, knowledge-based economy, but we still have to sit and sleep somewhere. Offering a full range of lifestyle choices in a metropolitan area, both the predominant drivable sub-urban pattern *and* the walkable urban pattern, is more important now than ever in attracting and retaining an educated workforce. If the lifestyle choice of walkable urbanism is not offered, many businesses and households will settle elsewhere. As consumer surveys in downtown Philadelphia and Detroit in 2006 have shown, this seems to be particularly true for the well-educated, who seem to have a predilection for living in walkable urban places.[6] In 2006, twenty-five percent of Americans over twenty-five years of age had a college degree. The new residents in reviving downtown Detroit and Philadelphia were more than eighty percent college-educated.

This book explores how we came to the place during the last half of the twentieth century that the only development option was drivable sub-urbanism. This historically new, radical, and seemingly superior way of living resulted in an overreaction, pushing the pendulum of development all the way to the opposite end of the continuum for decades. It is certainly desirable for many people, especially during certain parts of their lifetimes. However, making it the only option offered in American metropolitan areas takes a good thing too far.

I look into the roots of this social experiment in transportation, law, housing, and finance that created exponential outward growth in where we built our homes, shops, and offices. This bold and large-scale social experiment was not some nefarious conspiracy; Americans have willingly engaged in it. In fact, drivable sub-urbanism aligned with the basic drivers of the economy: car manufacturing, the oil industry, and highway-based infrastructure development. Drivable sub-urbanism helped to create more economic wealth for the country and became integral to the mid- to late-twentieth century version of the American Dream.

As we shall see, this experiment has been going on so long that much of the real estate and financial industries know how to finance and build only drivable sub-urban development. We now have a financing system and construction technology that makes so many communities today look so much alike. The experiment also solidified into a system of subsidies that we continue to pay today. There have been many unforeseen, generally negative, consequences of investing thirty-five percent of our country's wealth in building only drivable sub-urbanism. These unintended consequences include geometric increases in land consumption, the decline of community, and a proven correlation with the increasing rates of obesity and asthma. And the consequences are worldwide. The country's foreign policy in the Middle East is partially driven by the need for oil to power our cars. The connection between drivable sub-urban development and greenhouse gas emissions is just about intuitive.

THE RE-EMERGENCE OF WALKABLE URBANISM

However, the bigger story here is about future market demand—the revival of walkable urbanism and the promise it holds for our communities. The pendulum that swung wildly from one extreme to the other seems to be coming back toward the middle, due to changing demographics, changing consumer preferences, and our increasing knowledge of the unintended negative consequences of relying on a single development pattern. Some contemporary metropolitan observers characterize American and worldwide sprawling land patterns as a continuing progression throughout history of ever more spread out development. Society must recognize a more complex and varied pattern.

Many Americans are learning that there is another way of life—one that does not include spending hours in traffic jams each day. That paying nearly as much to own and operate the family fleet of cars as we pay to own our home is not a way to build wealth. That getting unintentional exercise while walking to the store or work, seeing neighbors along the way, might be a better way for some to live. In addition, walkable urban places are far more environmentally sustainable because the number of cars required per household and the number of miles they are driven are substantially reduced. The higher density buildings are also inherently more environmentally friendly, using less energy for heating and cooling than stand-alone buildings. This also offers an economic benefit because more household income can be put into an appreciating asset (e.g., one's house) rather than depreciating assets (e.g., one's cars).

We face substantial hurdles to overcome in building new walkable urban places, in spite of the apparent pent-up demand. The walkable alternative is generally contrary to zoning codes; it is difficult to finance and baffling to build for much of the development industry due to its relative complexity. Also, drivable sub-urban development is substantially subsidized through subtle underwriting of infrastructure that costs more per house or commercial building when built at low density than at higher density, yet most times everyone pays about the same, no matter their neighborhood density. This means that compact urban development subsidizes low-density drivable sub-urbanism.

However, if the market wants something, it generally gets it. And a growing number of developers, investors, and planners are trying to build walkable urban development in spite of the legal, financial, and management obstacles and the subsidies for the competition. Making it possible for more communities to do so is the focus of the last third of the book, particularly through changes in financing, investment, and governance.

This book explains why and how the *next* American Dream is emerging. The next American Dream is not based upon nostalgic memory of what we have lost—the memory of 1955 Hill Valley—in our rush to build drivable sub-urban development. Nor is it just the recognition that the unintended consequences of 1985 Hill Valley, drivable sub-urbanism, including a myriad of social, environmental, fiscal, and economic issues, need to be addressed and solved. The next American Dream is based upon the recognition that the market wants a built environment that provides choice, lines up with the new economy that is emerging and is more environmentally, fiscally, and economically sustainable. This book also points out some of the probable unintended consequences of this next American Dream—it wouldn't be fair if we didn't leave our grandchildren some problems to solve.

1

FUTURAMA AND THE 20ᵀᴴ-CENTURY AMERICAN DREAM

Imagine yourself living a middle-class life in 1939 in one of America's cities, such as Philadelphia, Chicago, or Seattle. The Depression seems to be abating somewhat as the unemployment rate is down to *only* seventeen percent, compared to a staggering twenty-three percent of the workforce in the early part of the decade.[1] (For comparison, unemployment was 4.5 percent in 2006).[2] You probably live in a row house, apartment, or small single-family home, walking and taking the streetcar or subway most places because the family has only one car. The neighborhood is close in every sense of the term: you overhear much of what goes on next door and privacy is at a premium, but a sense of community is generally taken for granted. Daily shopping needs (figure 1.1) are satisfied by walking to the local A&P market, the Rexall drug store, and the Woolworth's five-and-dime, which are about five blocks away, as well as a variety of local merchants for candy, gifts, work or school clothes, and simple meals such as hamburgers. You know most of the merchants and they know you, even at the national chain stores. For important shopping, such as dress clothes and jewelry, or for banking, legal assistance, live theater, and white-tablecloth restaurants, you go

FIGURE 1.1. Prior to the Depression in the 1930s, it was common for local retailers, such as the A&P grocery, other national chains, and locally owned stores, to locate within a few blocks' walk of most houses. (Source: Philadelphia City Archives)

downtown (figure 1.2), which is a trolley or subway ride away, costing a nickel. The family bread winner also commutes to work by the trolley or subway.

If your family is working class, your life is somewhat although not fundamentally different. You also have retailers who know you within walking distance and transit access to downtown, although you probably have fewer reasons to go there even if you can afford the legitimate and illicit pleasures it offers. Your residence is likely to be within walking distance or a trolley ride away from the family breadwinner's workplace. Working-class housing surrounding manufacturing districts is a typical pattern (figure 1.3), because fewer working-class families have cars. Although convenient, the proximity of heavy manufacturing means your neighborhood

FIGURE 1.2. Downtown, where all the lights are bright and the sidewalks are crowded. (Source: Temple University Libraries, Urban Archives, Philadelphia)

is noisy, polluted, and smelly. Housing is much more cramped than in a middle-class home, putting privacy at even more of a premium.

Overall, both the middle-class and working-class families probably feel like everyday life is confined—a little too close for comfort. Although

FIGURE 1.3. Good news/bad news story: Much working-class employment was only a few blocks away from home. (Source: Print and Picture Collection, The Free Library of Philadelphia)

the likelihood of war in Europe is great in 1939, the economic storm clouds of the Depression seem finally to be lifting and you have reason to hope for a better day for the country's economy and your own standard of living.

THE WORLD OF TOMORROW

If you were lucky enough to go to the New York City World's Fair in the summer of 1939 or 1940, you would have seen an entirely different way of living. According to the official guide book, the World's Fair would give a "graphic demonstration to the dream of a better 'World of Tomorrow,'" the theme of the fair. Battered by the Depression and living with anxiety about the brewing war, Americans were ready for a new vision of how to live, work, and play; in essence, they were ready for a new version of the American Dream. The fair attracted 45 million people, setting the all-time record for world's fair attendance.[3, 4]

FIGURE 1.4. Looking down on "the many wonders that may develop in the not too distant future . . . the wonderful world of 1960!" at the Futurama exhibit. (Source: Copyright 2007 GM Corp. Used with permission, GM Media Archive)

The highlight of the fair was in the "The Highways and Horizons" exhibit, better known as Futurama (figure 1.4). You had to wait in line at least an hour and maybe even two. According to the authoritative commentator's voice booming out of the hidden speakers in the exhibit's 600 moving chairs, Futurama offered "a magic Aladdin-like flight through time and space . . . of the many wonders that may develop in the not too distant future . . . the wonderful world of 1960!"[5] Finally, you were carried along an indoor ride looking at a toy-train-size model of the American countryside and cities. To twenty-first-century eyes, looking at a model—even a football-field-size model with tiny moving cars—does not inspire much excitement. But for our parents, grandparents, and great-grandparents in the late 1930s, it was wondrous.

Futurama was the most popular exhibit of the fair, drawing more than 27 million visitors.[6] About ten percent of the country's population may have seen the Futurama vision of the "world of tomorrow" (subtracting those who probably saw it multiple times and international visitors).[7] As Brendan Nee wrote in *The Planning Legacy of World's Fairs,* "the exhibit that stole the show was the 'Futurama' exhibit." Most other Americans read about it in the many magazine articles that focused on the exhibit, such as the June 5, 1939, issue of *Life* magazine, which had the theme "America's Future" in keeping with the theme of the fair. *Life* had a five-page spread on Futurama. There is no way to accurately measure the impact of Futurama on public opinion, government policy, and the built environment. But as Corn and Horrigan commented in their book, *Yesterday's Tomorrows: Past Visions of the American Future,* "no futuristic film or exhibit [has] ever been so convincing" as Futurama.[8]

THE NEW DREAM OF DRIVABLE SUB-URBANISM

The real focus of Futurama was roads: "superhighways" and the greatly expanded and fundamentally different metropolitan areas that would be built as a result of those roads. Futurama showed radio-controlled, automated fourteen-lane highways crisscrossing the country with three speed limits (depending on the lane) of fifty, seventy-five, and one hundred miles per hour.

In the world of Futurama, gone were the busy streets where cars, trolleys, and people competed for space and sidewalks were so crowded that pedestrians seemed to be pushed along by the crowd. Gone were the high-density apartments and townhouses built right up to the sidewalks.

In their place in the distant future of 1960, American suburbs offered homes with attached garages and spacious yards. Downtowns had new high-rise office buildings, hotels, and a few apartment buildings separated from one another by those wide roads as well as large structured parking decks next to each building. The Futurama-inspired downtown of 1960 would have pedestrian sidewalks elevated above the cars, which were on the ground level.

The designer of Futurama was Norman Bel Geddes, one of the leading industrial designers of the day. In the companion book to Futurama, *Magic Motorways*, he delighted in poking fun at the walkable urbanism of the day with a pixie sense of humor,[9] for example, suggesting that Greenwich Village was laid out by meandering cows. His goal was "accelerating city traffic one hundred percent" by removing obstacles such as rotaries; his example was Dupont Circle in Washington, D.C., where "danger lies where paths cross." His automatic, long distance "magic motorways,"[10] which would connect and ring metropolitan areas, would link to nonstop urban freeways.

As fair-goers emerged from the ride (figure 1.5), they found themselves in a life-size replica of an intersection they had just seen in the model. They were at the elevated pedestrian level of a real intersection with a six-lane one-way street crammed with automobiles below them at ground level. They had stepped from a dreamscape into reality, reinforcing that dreams of the future can come true. The last words they heard from the commentator was "***all eyes to the future***."

Futurama inspired a vision of postwar America that became the unchallenged assumption of how to construct the built environment. E.B. White, writing about Futurama for *Harper's* magazine, had a nearly spiritual reaction. "A ride on the Futurama . . . induces approximately the same emotional response as a trip through the Cathedral of St. John the Divine. I didn't want to wake up. I liked 1960 in purple lights, going a hundred miles an hour around impossible turns ever onwards toward the certified cities of the flawless future."[11]

There was little debate about whether the future should be car-driven. The excitement for this vision drowned out the few critics such as great urbanist Lewis Mumford, who wrote in the July 1939 *New Yorker* that these roads would "cancel out the motorist's freedom of speed and movement . . . [reducing] driving to a chore."[12]

The company responsible for Futurama had good reason to promote a car-based future riding on a superhighway system, presumably paid for

FIGURE 1.5. Following the ten-minute ride overlooking the Futurama model, visitors emerged into a full-sized replica of the 1960 intersection they had just seen in the model, complete with the new lineup of GM cars. Pedestrians were separated from the cars on the street below. This exhibit helped demonstrate that the Futurama vision could come true. (Source: Copyright 2007 GM Corp. Used with permission, GM Media Archive)

by taxpayer dollars. The sponsor was the largest car manufacturer on the planet, General Motors (GM).[13]

The extremely influential Walter Lippmann said that "GM has spent a small fortune to convince the American public that if it wishes to enjoy the full benefit of private enterprise in motor manufacturing, it will have to rebuild its cities and highways by public enterprise."[14] As Brendan Lee said in *The Planning Legacy of World's Fairs,* Futurama "no doubt helped to influence the public perception of a publicly funded superhighway system and a society of automobile ownership."[15] In essence, GM and the rest of the auto-industrial complex, supported by the general public sentiment of the day, wanted the thirty-five percent of the assets of the

American economy invested in a fundamentally different way than prior to the Depression.

IMPLEMENTING THE FUTURAMA VISION

Futurama seemed to plant a visual and emotional seed in the American consciousness that germinated during the war years (1941 to 1945). There was little anyone could do immediately about satisfying the hope of a different and better life because the war effort was all-consuming. More than forty percent of the gross domestic product (GDP) at the war's peak went to the war effort (compared to under four percent of GDP for defense spending in 2005). Car production stopped completely during the early 1940s, because the auto industry shifted to the production of military equipment. The building industry stalled, as construction dropped to the lowest level of development in the twentieth century. This continued the similarly low levels of housing and commercial real estate development from the 1930s, when most of the private real estate industry had been in hibernation due to the Depression. New housing starts were more than sixty percent lower during the Depression years and the Second World War than in the 1920s.[16] By 1945, it had been half a generation since there was anything resembling normalcy in new housing and commercial growth.

This resulted in the build up of tremendous pent-up demand that exploded after the war ended in 1945 for all types of housing and commercial development—the consequence of marriages, divorces, births, deaths, new jobs, and every other demographic and economic change that continually occur in society. There was also plenty of spending power, because most consumer goods had been rationed during the war, driving up savings rates. Annual new housing production shot up and stayed up. Annual new housing starts were four times greater on average from 1946 to 1960 compared to 1930 to 1945, the years of the Depression and the Second World War.[17] The pent-up demand and demographic changes, particularly the start of the Baby Boom, were compounded by the hunger for a different, better, and richly deserved life after the end of the twin traumas of the Depression and the war. The image effectively planted by Futurama and reinforced by magazines, news reels, movies, and other mass media promised a future unlike the recent past. It was an image of a new American Dream of one's family living in a detached house on one's own plot of land with increased privacy, a car to drive there, and superhighways to commute to work.[18] This was entirely different than any society ever built in history.

THE PREINDUSTRIAL WALKING CITY

Cities first arose in Sumer, located in present-day Iraq, about 5,500 years ago. From Sumer until the industrial revolution in the nineteenth century, all cities were driven by similar day-to-day transportation systems, which were walkable, horse-drawn, and sometimes waterborne. For example, most streets of Roman Pompeii were eighteen to twenty-four feet wide from building front to building front and allowed for narrow elevated sidewalks on both sides of a depressed cart path. This transportation system, which was both walkable and horse-drawn, dictated that the vast majority of dwellings and businesses were close together due to the limited range a pedestrian or even a horse could conveniently travel for everyday commuting. Only a few of the well-to-do were able to live outside the city walls in suburban villas, and these may have been second homes with primary homes in town.

Jump forward to preindustrial seventeenth century London of diarist Samuel Pepys's day and you would find a very similar layout, except that there was a navigable river, which added rowboats and sailboats as means to get around. The basic layout, street configuration, and density of Pompeii and Renaissance London were basically the same. Both are examples of walkable urbanism.

In Kenneth Jackson's magisterial work, *Crabgrass Frontier,* he stressed the walkability of preindustrial cities. "In 1815, even in the largest cities, only about one person in fifty traveled as much as a mile to his place of employment. . . . Because any distance has to be overcome by horse or foot, there was a significant advantage in living within easy walking distance of the city's stores and businesses."[19]

In the nineteenth century with the beginnings of the industrial era, commuter and elevated trains, steam ferries, omnibuses, and cable cars began to tremendously expand the reach of cities; however, the compact form around the many new stations remained essentially the same as before. The new forms of transportation radiated out of the city center, allowing far more people to enjoy life in the suburbs or "uptown." Yet, once commuters got to their home station, they still only had their feet or a waiting horse to get them to their home. This transportation reality kept these new suburban places compact. For example, commuter railroad suburbs became the rage in the late nineteenth and early twentieth centuries. In the United States, the many stops along the Main Line outside Philadelphia, the North Shore of Chicago, and the Mid-Peninsula south of San Francisco were developed as small, walkable downtowns, each similar to 1955 downtown Hill Valley in the film *Back to the Future*.

THE TRANSFORMATION OF THE AMERICAN DREAM

The American Dream, defined by Cal Jillson in *Pursuing the American Dream,* is "a shimmering vision of a fruitful country open to all who come, learn, work, save, invest, and play by the rules."[20] However, the American Dream has been played out on the ground in different ways at different times, based upon the economic underpinnings of the country at the time. The eighteenth and nineteenth century version of the American Dream could be summarized by the phrase "forty acres and a mule." It was inspired by the Jeffersonian image of the country being populated by "yeoman farmers," which was appropriate for the economy of the time. After all, eighty-three percent of all jobs were in agriculture in 1800, when Jefferson was elected president, and more than ninety percent of Americans lived in rural areas of the country, not in the "walking city," as described by Jackson in *Crabgrass Frontier.*[21] Agricultural jobs still represented forty percent of all jobs 100 years later in 1900 and remained the largest category of jobs in the economy. More than sixty percent of Americans were still living on farms in 1900.[22] This rural version of the American Dream dominated the nineteenth century and the early twentieth century.

The Jeffersonian agricultural ideal has been a persistent part of how the American Dream plays out on the ground. Jefferson had a well-known dislike for cities and the manufacturers and financiers who populated their upper ranks. One of his famous quotes could not make his distain for cities more clear: "I think our governments will remain virtuous for many centuries as long as they are chiefly agricultural. . . . When they get plied upon one another in large cities, as in Europe, they will become corrupt as in Europe."[23]

Cities were (justifiably) viewed as dangerous, smelly, toxic places in the nineteenth century. There was also the fear of the constant waves of immigrants, whether from Europe, Asia, or blacks from the American South. Cities have generally been the port of entry for the influx of immigrants throughout American history; disdain for and racist sentiment toward each new immigrant group is as American as apple pie.

It was in the early twentieth century that the first shift in American history occurred in the definition of how the American Dream played out on the ground. The shift was from an agricultural ideal to a suburban ideal, though still based upon a common Jeffersonian disdain for cities. This second version of the American Dream manifested itself far differently than the agricultural version in its effect on the built environment, because a suburban subdivision obviously is laid out on the ground far differently than is a farm. However, this change showed that the American Dream is not immutable; its physical development could be fundamentally modified.

In 1920, manufacturing jobs caught up with agricultural jobs; each sector had about twenty-six percent of the total jobs in the economy. This signaled the shift to the then *new* economy, the industrial economy, which was primarily based in metropolitan areas. In the 1920 U.S. Census, for the first time in American history, a majority of Americans were living in metropolitan areas, not in rural areas.[24]

Manufacturing jobs stayed at about twenty-six percent of all U.S. jobs until 1970, the peak of the industrial economy. But it was not just an industrial economy, it was a car-based industrial economy.[25] At the 1970s peak, the automotive sector of the economy (car manufacturing and suppliers) held 1.7 percent of all jobs and accounted for two percent of the economy.[26] However, these figures do not count the other sectors of the economy necessary for automotive manufacturing, maintenance, operations, and finance—the oil industry, steel, mining, car sales and repair, car finance and insurance, road building and repair, etc., which multiplies those totals many times.[27] In total, the direct impact of automobile manufacturing and the many ancillary businesses was at least ten percent of all jobs at its peak and, therefore, possibly a third of all jobs when the indirect impact (the "ripple effect") is considered. It is likely that the production and operation of cars literally drove the American economy for most of the middle years of the twentieth century as the Futurama vision was being implemented. In 1953, when President of GM Charles E. Wilson sat before the Senate at his confirmation hearing to be Secretary of Defense and said that "what was good for the country was good for General Motors and vice versa," *it was true.*

A car manufacturing economic development strategy is not exclusively American; like many economic and social trends of the past century, the United States just happened to follow it first. The Japanese followed this same strategy, starting in the 1960s, followed by Korea in the 1990s. China is following this well-trodden path in the 2000s as they add car manufacturing as a key component of their phenomenal growth strategy.

The car-based industrial economy changed how the American Dream was built, driven by drivable sub-urbanism. If we would just "see the USA in your Chevrolet," we would help both our families' and our country's economic prospects. Psychologically, practically, and for economic growth reasons, Americans wanted to be driven by the car and craved the freedom, flexibility, privacy, comfort, reliability, speed, sexiness, and individuality it offered. The agricultural economy paid for the Jeffersonian rural ideal—the American Dream of the day. Likewise, the car-driven industrial economy paid for the drivable sub-urban ideal, the American Dream of the mid- to late twentieth century.

IMPLEMENTING FUTURAMA

Futurama did not just spring whole from the mind of Norman Bel Geddes or from the marketing department at General Motors. It was part of a movement led by modernists such as Le Corbusier, Walter Gropius, Mies van de Rohe, and Ludwig Hilberseimer.[28] These men believed that new technologies, particularly the automobile, could and should transform city life. Their ideas transformed both architecture and city form around the world. In the United States, the pent-up demand for change after the Second World War proved fertile ground for these new ideas. The result was a de facto domestic policy that produced a massive social engineering experiment: the implementation of the Futurama vision.

The uniqueness of the Futurama social engineering experiment was its scale and boldness. Combining federal, state, and local laws, subsidy programs, and infrastructure investments encouraged and in actuality mandated only one kind of growth: low-density, drivable sub-urbanism. This American domestic policy has been dictating growth for the past sixty years and is still in force in the early twenty-first century.

From one perspective, any domestic policy engages in social engineering. Whether it is the tax deductibility of home mortgages to increase home ownership, tax-deductible charitable contributions to encourage donations, or laws to try to keep citizens from buying illicit drugs, domestic policy is social engineering. The social engineering that promoted drivable sub-urbanism was not a conspiracy imposed on the American people; we wanted it and we truly believed it to be the best future.

Federal programs sprang up during the 1930s Depression, but particularly after the Second World War, to encourage single-family housing in the car-accessible suburbs of the postwar era. These included housing loan insurance programs by the Federal Housing Administration (FHA) in 1934 for moderate-income households and by the Veterans Administration (VA) for returning soldiers in 1944. These programs allowed for mortgages that conformed to certain standards, which, due to regulatory guidelines and to racial discriminatory practices known as "redlining" (the marking of a map in red ink indicating areas where these programs were not allowed due to the preponderance of racial minorities), gave preference to newly constructed, single-family homes in white suburbs. (These racial provisions were outlawed by the Supreme Court in 1948, although the FHA did not stop accepting them until 1950.)[29] Rehabilitation of existing urban homes and high-density attached housing was not allowable under VA or FHA financing schemes. Given that a quarter of all home loans had VA or FHA insurance between 1950 and 1970,[30] this meant that only suburban low-density housing would be federally insured, hence subsidized.[31]

Another government policy that has favored drivable sub-urban development took hold at the local level through zoning codes, first implemented in 1916 in New York City. In the industrial economy of the early and mid-twentieth century, when zoning was initially put in place, the intent was to separate uses (e.g., housing from workplace, retail from residential, etc.); who wanted to live near dirty, noisy, polluting factories? All of this was to obtain the eternal goal of planners of the day—"plenty of light and air." The result was to keep different uses separate from one another, and when bigger buildings had to be built, to make sure they were spaced farther apart with grassy lawns in between and with ample parking for residents and visitors.

The current definitive study of the effect of zoning on land use patterns is by Jonathan Levine in his 2005 book, Zoned Out.[32] "The empirical evidence suggests that the 'American way of zoning' truly does make the suburbs of U.S. metropolitan areas more spread out than they would otherwise be. . . . Land development markets are capable of producing more compact development than is currently observed but are thwarted by municipal regulation." Zoning has had the effect of limiting choice to the market.

An example is Santa Fe, New Mexico, which has one of the most dense and successful small-city downtowns in the country. Within its downtown and the extension of the downtown, art gallery–packed Canyon Road, there are 650 shops, thousands of hotel rooms, City Hall, office buildings, and high-density condominiums and small-lot, single-family houses. The city, founded in 1609, was laid out according to the Law of the Indies, propagated by King Phillip II of Spain as a template for all Spanish towns and cities in the New World. As a result of following this pattern of walkable urbanism, Santa Fe has become one of the most beloved cities in the country for residents, second-home residents, and the 2 million annual visitors. Yet, if the downtown were to tragically burn down, the current zoning codes would legally allow only low-density, car-oriented strip commercial development to take its place. Obviously there would be "variances," special legislation requiring city council approval to set aside zoning laws if such a massive rebuilding were to take place. But the proscribed law for development in Santa Fe would produce "anywhere USA" strip retail, similar to the locally "dreaded" Cerrillos Road, not the present downtown of the "City Different."

FUTURAMA TAKES TO THE ROAD

The most obvious program of the Futurama-inspired domestic policy was the Federal-Aid Highway Act of 1956, also known as the National Interstate and Defense Highways Act, which built the 46,837-mile system that was finally finished in 1991.[33] Although there were many reasons for the passage of this act, including increasing mobility for national defense; encouraging the building and connecting of the country's commercial truck transportation network; creating jobs; and supporting manufacturing, trucking, and construction companies and labor unions, it was based upon the unchallenged assumption of a car-based transportation system.[34] Building the Interstate Highway System was the largest construction project undertaken in American history in physical size, social impact, and cost. And unlike other developed countries' highway systems, it came into and through most large American cities, rather than terminating at a ring road or transitioning onto city streets, as was the case in most European cities. American highways provided both inter-metropolitan transportation *and* intra-metropolitan area transportation. This allowed the new highway system to not only link the nation together but to link the city to the surrounding countryside, allowing low-density, decentralized housing subdivisions to spring up. The Futurama vision could be realized.

Government regulations and policies massively subsidized drivable sub-urbanism. This took the form of outright grants and matching grants for roads, particularly the Interstate Highway System (generally eighty to ninety percent federal funding), sewer and water systems, the building of public schools, the continuation of FHA and VA loan programs, and drainage and flood protection. Initially paid by federal and state taxpayers, infrastructure was extended almost exclusively to low-density, fringe development. Rehabilitation of existing infrastructure was effectively barred. For example, until recently, national educational guidelines and state education department standards for school construction recommended very generous minimum acreage standards for school playing fields and parking lots. For high schools, the recommendation was thirty acres of land; one acre was recommended for every 100 students. Rehabilitation of existing schools had to meet a high hurdle to prove it would be cost-effective.[35] This meant that new schools were the norm, and they had to be sited at the edge of town on former farmland or open space where everyone had to be bused or driven, or had to drive themselves.[36] Although the national standards have been relaxed, many states have not yet changed their requirements.

Kenneth Jackson's *Crabgrass Frontier* concluded that the federal role in the domestic land use policy was "enormous." The federal government's transportation policy was "emphasizing and benefiting the road, the truck and the private motorcar." The FHA, according to Jackson, "had a more pervasive and powerful impact on the American people over the past half century (1934 until 1984)" than any other agency of the federal government. Combining the transportation investments, finance, and infrastructure subsidies with legal zoning codes prescribing drivable sub-urban development and prohibiting anything else results in a powerful domestic policy.

EFFECT ON EXISTING CITIES

The implementation of the Futurama-inspired domestic policy had a major impact on the economic and fiscal health of central cities; most virtually collapsed, both socially and financially. Their mayors became beggars in pursuit of handouts from their state legislatures and the federal government. Virtually every downtown was in absolute and relative decline, virtually no housing being built in the center city, office space growing at half the rate required to maintain regional market share, industrial zones being abandoned, and retail almost completely deserting the downtown for the suburbs. Most downtown department stores were closed by the end of the 1980s. The middle class left most center cities, leaving only the poor, who have the most social welfare needs and the least financial ability to pay the taxes to support these services.

Certainly there were much-publicized efforts at revitalization; the Johnson administration launched the Model Cities program and urban renewal in the 1960s, city planners in the 1970s closed main streets to pretend the city was a suburban mall, and in the 1980s the federal government handed out Urban Development Action Grants. These programs had limited success at best, and most failed to achieve their objectives of returning center cities to health. Over time, these programs were putting *billions* of dollars into cities, but the cities were offering a kind of lifestyle the market did not want at the time. These individual programs could not effectively counteract the transportation policies, subsidies, and financial guarantees that over time directed *trillions* of dollars of infrastructure investment into what most Americans wanted: drivable sub-urban development.

As we implemented the Futurama vision, virtually no destination was walkable for a practical reason. Drivable sub-urbanism may include sidewalks and paths, but they generally do not go anywhere meaningful for day-to-day life, such as a grocery store, work, or school. The distances are far too great, there are serious barriers such as freeways and wide, busy streets, and it is generally unpleasant and unsafe to walk in a drivable sub-urban place once outside the residential districts. Anyone walking in commercial drivable sub-urban districts, such as strip retail areas, is actually considered suspicious today.

The very low development densities in drivable sub-urban development also make any form of rail transit and most bus transit impractical. Current drivable sub-urban densities would have to increase more than *six times* to make transit work.

The promise of the Futurama exhibit helped launched an interlocking system of policies and subsidies that unwittingly pushed aside all historical precedents in city building and produced the car-only, drivable sub-urban pattern of growth. It is the land use equivalent of the supposed Henry Ford dictate that the buyer can have a Model T "in any color, so long as it's black." In the next two chapters, we will see how this system played out on the ground and in the real estate industry to produce more and more "black Model Ts."

2

THE RISE OF DRIVABLE SUB-URBIA

Walkable urbanism was not what the returning World War II veterans and the home-front families wanted. It seemed old-fashioned and not in keeping with the exciting new world that Futurama promised. The pent-up demand for drivable sub-urbanism was over-whelming, and it was in relatively short supply at the time.

As the zoning, housing, and transportation subsidies for drivable sub-urbanism began to fall into place, metropolitan areas started to change radically. Each decade after the Second World War, a different layering of new development moved into place. In each of these decades, different kinds of real estate products, such as housing or retail, began to migrate out from the core city. The physical size of our metropolitan areas expanded geometrically, just as Norman Bel Geddes had forecast; however, his Futurama vision did not happen in the center city but in the suburbs, where the blank slate of green fields beckoned.

TRANSPORTATION DRIVES DEVELOPMENT

Although the zoning and housing finance systems and subsidies were important to implementing the Futurama vision, the new vision of transportation provided by the Interstate Highway System was the primary catalyst for this major transformation. Throughout urban history, transportation has driven development. The transportation system in which the society chooses to invest its money, either direct government dollars or government-regulated private dollars, is the primary dictator of where and how we construct the built environment.[1]

Developers had plenty of space to build because the United States has never suffered from a shortage of land. Only one percent of all land was urbanized in 1945, where nearly two-thirds of Americans then lived.[2] When the independent and flexible means of transport provided by the car was employed for part or all of a commute, running errands or going to school, a tremendous amount of acreage could be reached. For example, most people give themselves twenty to thirty minutes to commute each way from work to home, with the national average being 24.3 minutes.[3] A twenty-four–minute automobile commute, traveling at an average of thirty miles an hour, is twelve miles. Assuming one's place of employment helps determine where to live, a twelve-mile radius from work encompasses 463 square miles, a little less than half the size of Rhode Island (1,045 square miles). This huge radius for drivable suburban housing development is the main force that promotes sprawl. A one-mile increase in the drivable radius adds three-fold to land area, and a ten-mile increase adds 100-fold.

Although the car seems to offer unbounded freedom, in fact the car-based transportation system *decreases* transportation flexibility. A decentralized transportation system allows only cars to connect work to home, home to shopping, and home to school. Transit, bicycling, and walking become less and less viable, pleasant, and safe as development spreads out. As mentioned in chapter 1, current suburban densities would have to increase about *six times* to make any sort of transit work.

DEVELOPMENT DRIVERS AND FOLLOWERS

How this newfound flexibility provided by the car played out on the ground was driven by the real estate product types that can be classified as either "drivers" or "followers." Driver product types include housing, major entertainment/cultural venues (arenas, stadiums, performing arts centers, museums), universities, and regional and national hospitals. Drivers have the largest drawing radius: the entertainment venues draw from the entire metropolitan area, whereas, housing, as explained above, has a ten- to fifteen-mile drawing radius in a drivable sub-urban environment (less than a mile in a walkable urban place). Followers include neighborhood-serving retail, restaurants, office space, and self storage. Follower products must have the sources of demand, primarily residential units ("rooftops" in the jargon), in place before these products are built. For most neighborhood-serving follower land uses, the drawing radius is two to three miles in a drivable sub-urban environment (under one mile in a walkable urban environment). Somewhere in between driver and follower products are those that must have some demand in place before they open, and the developers and tenants are confident the market will fill in quickly. Those in-between products include regional-serving office and industrial development, big-box power centers (clusters of big-box stores), regional malls, and hotels. I have found that the drawing radius of these products in a drivable sub-urban environment tends to be three to seven miles (one to three miles in a walkable urban environment).

As the initial limited-access highways were being built, it was housing that led the way to the suburbs. Housing (for-sale and rental) represents fifty-six percent of the built environment (nonresidential income real estate is twenty-eight percent and infrastructure is sixteen percent), which makes it the largest category of the built environment.[4] In the five years between 1946 and 1950 more than *three* times as many houses were built per year than during the fifteen years of the Depression and the war (1930 to 1945).[5] The 1950s saw a *four-fold* increase over the Depression and the war years in annual housing production. This was the largest increase in housing production in the nation's history in both percentage and absolute terms.[6]

Neighborhood-serving retail was the first to follow housing out to the suburbs beginning in the 1950s and accelerating in the 1960s.

Neighborhood-serving retail includes drug stores, stationery stores, casual restaurants, fast food restaurants, and most importantly, grocery stores. Most every one of us ends up in a grocery store with some frequency, so it acts as the ultimate anchor for a neighborhood-serving retail center. The new shopping centers in the 1950s took a transitional form. The 1920s shopping areas were built to be accessible on foot or by trolley or bus. Because a minority of people drove and hence had to park their cars, these areas were designed to accommodate only a few cars. When retail centers were being built again in the 1950s, they were designed and built to be walkable, based on the 1920s model, but allowances were made for the greater percentage of customers who were arriving by car. Some parallel or angled parking was placed in front of the stores for a few lucky souls, and many more spaces were found in a surface parking lot in the back of the stores, generally connected by a covered walkway. (It is interesting to note that many of these 1950s centers have found new life in the first decade of the twenty-first century because this design seems to fit the "back to the future" market realities of today, as will be discussed in chapter 8).

However, beginning in the 1960s, the growing need for almost everyone to drive to neighborhood-serving retail caused architects and builders to push the stores to the extreme back of the property, allowing all of the parking spaces to be in front of the stores; the classic drivable sub-urban commercial development pattern was born. This setback of retail and all other forms of commercial development to allow for clearly seen and accessible parking changed everything; it meant that almost no one would or could walk to the store again. Any pedestrian would need to brave a very unpleasant walk on an isolated sidewalk (assuming there was a sidewalk at all) immediately adjacent to rushing traffic, and walk through a large and not very pedestrian-safe parking lot, only to have to repeat the trip with full shopping bags to get home. New retail formats also pushed more of the storage of goods on to the consumer, making a shopping trip to the grocery store a weekly affair with more goods purchased at one time. It was not possible to walk anywhere with so many groceries.

With neighborhood-serving retail thriving in this new car-oriented shopping center form in the 1960s, it took little time for the regional-serving retailers, land uses in between drivers and followers, to join the trend. Regional retail, particularly department stores, still concentrated downtown to a large extent during the initial postwar period. A few pioneering department stores ventured into the wilds of suburbia in the 1950s, building stand-alone stores not connected to other stores. They soon learned the power that they had.

In the 1960s developers built the first regional malls, initially uncovered. They were an immediate hit. Department stores began to anchor regional malls and attracted other stores that wanted to reach the customers making the trip for these anchor stores. As a result, department stores could obtain tremendous economic concessions from the regional mall developer because they had a proven customer base. These initial department stores in the suburbs were "branches" of the main store that was still downtown in the 1960s. By the late 1980s, most downtown department stores had closed and the mall branches became the main stores.

In the 1970s, regional-serving retail staged a mass exodus from downtown as housing subdivisions continued to spread to the ever-expanding metropolitan fringe, followed by more neighborhood-serving retail. With more traffic congestion created by all of this housing and retail activity, highway infrastructure had to keep up. The expanded highway capacity opened the way for the next phase of drivable sub-urban development: office and industrial jobs. In the 1970s the first serious growth of office and industrial space in the suburbs began a massive relocation of businesses and jobs from near or in the traditional downtown of the region. These relocations and the new jobs they created went exactly where the limited-access highways were and, significantly, close to the upper-income housing concentration.

RISE OF THE FAVORED QUARTER

These housing and retail trends began to reveal a new and unexpected metropolitan development trend. Each metro area began to grow in a single predominant direction: the "favored quarter," a ninety-degree arc that starts in the traditional downtown of the major city in the region and fans outward in one direction. It is favored because so much infrastructure investment has been bestowed on it, thereby guaranteeing its dominance in regional economic growth. It is favored because it is the wealthiest portion of the metropolitan area and because the vast majority of relocating and new jobs land in the favored quarter.

The idealized map in figure 2.1 shows how the growth from the 1950s through the 1980s played out on the ground in the typical American metropolitan area. Looking for the limited-access highways, the concentration of upper-income housing to the east in this map and the local minority housing to the west, the bulge to the east—the favored quarter—is obvious. The direction of growth for the favored quarter is different in each metropolitan area. In Atlanta, Dallas, and Orlando, the favored quarter goes north. In Phoenix, Seattle, and St. Paul, the favored quarter goes east. In Kansas City and Denver, the favored quarter goes south. The largest metropolitan areas in the country (New York City, Los Angeles, Chicago, San Francisco, Philadelphia, and Miami/Fort Lauderdale) have two or three favored quarters due to their size. For example, the growth coming out of New York City could not be confined to one direction, so it went east toward Long Island, northeast toward Connecticut, and southwest toward Princeton, New Jersey.

According to Al Taubman, the founder of Taubman Realty, Inc., one of the first and still one of the largest regional mall companies in the country, site selection in the early days was pretty easy. You built where the limited-access highways were being built, locating at an interchange as close to where the high-end shoppers lived as possible. Enabling high-end customers to get to the regional mall quickly and conveniently by car was the name of the game. In Philadelphia, that meant the first regional mall, the King of Prussia Mall, which opened in 1963, located at the intersection of the region's first limited-access highway, the newly built Schuylkill Freeway, and the Pennsylvania Turnpike. The King of Prussia Mall was just about in the middle of the Main Line, the largest

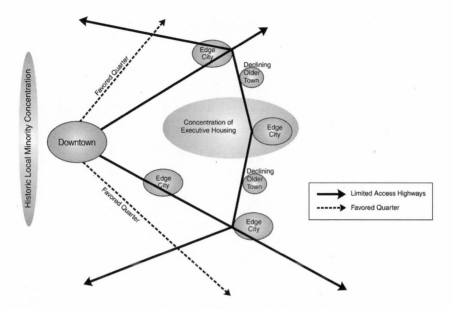

FIGURE 2.1. This idealized map shows the typical metropolitan area in the late 1980s. Knowing the locations of three items--the concentration of executive housing, which is generally white; the concentration of minority housing; and the limited access highways—leads to an understanding of the location of the favored quarter. This is where most infrastructure was built during the postwar period through the 1980s, most new jobs located, and many existing jobs relocated.

upper-income housing concentration of Philadelphia.[7] This pattern was followed throughout the country. The initial step toward the creation of the favored quarter was taken.

Many factors are cited in corporate surveys studying reasons for office job locations, such as access to customers, access to employees, prestigious address, and accessibility. However, talk to any office real estate developer, and you will find out that the number one reason is convenient access to the boss's house. This is part of the reason why by the first decade of the twenty-first century, seventy percent of all Washington, D.C., metropolitan office space is to the northwest of the city, the favored quarter, where approximately ninety percent of the region's housing valued at more than $1 million is located. This is why seventy percent of all Seattle metropolitan area office space is to the east of the city, the favored quarter, where seventy-five percent of the region's housing valued at more than $1 million is located.[8]

Another retail trend of the postwar era was the regionalization of local-serving retail—the emergence of regional-serving "category killer." These stores focused on electronics, appliances, books, music, hardware, home improvement, even midlevel dining. The rise of stores such as Circuit City, Borders Books, Home Depot, and Best Buy put formerly neighborhood-serving stores in their categories out of business by offering lower prices and wider selection, though much lower service levels. These stores were initially stand-alone, but eventually clustered together in power centers. This was another real estate product type added to the types in between driver and follower with a three- to five-mile drawing radius. Power centers meant that neighborhood-serving retail played less of a role in customers' lives and the commercial places in their neighborhoods.

THE FAVORED QUARTER AND RACIAL POLITICS

Race and poverty were big factors in the creation of the favored quarter. If you know three things about a metropolitan area, you can generally determine how it grew over the past half century and where the favored quarter is located. Those three factors are:

- where the concentration of high-income, generally white, households locate,
- where the historic concentration of low-income, generally minority, households locate, and
- where the limited-access highway system goes.

The first two of the three factors influencing the location of the favored quarter involve race, and the third is a reaction to the first two. The high-income housing is in the middle of the favored quarter, attracting growth. The local minority housing concentration is typically 180 degrees on the other side of the metro area from the high-income housing, assuming that the topography allows it, and where it does not, it is as far away as physically possible. The highway system is most extensively developed in the favored quarter, due to political and traffic pressures, to allow for ease of commuting around the favored quarter.

High-income housing clusters follow the "birds of a feather flock together" phenomenon.[9] The high-end housing clusters in most metropolitan areas, where seventy to ninety percent of this type of housing concentrates, allow better schools to be established and country clubs to be within close proximity of most members, and bestow prestige for living at the "right" address. High-end retailing naturally wants to be close to high-end shoppers, which meant that the early regional malls located in the favored quarter. The new freeways eased the increased traffic for this new retail.

Many new suburbs became political entities during the initial postwar period. Smaller suburban governments allowed households to cluster together in relatively homogeneous political jurisdictions. Racial, ethnic, and class concentrations existed before drivable sub-urbanism appeared on the scene, but not to the extent possible in the late twentieth century, as codified by political boundaries. As David Brooks said in his book, *On Paradise Drive,* "We all loudly declare our commitment to diversity, but in real life, we make strenuous efforts to find and fit in with people who make us feel comfortable."[10] This seems to work particularly well when political boundaries can be imposed to maintain homogeneity.

The jurisdictions in the favored quarter, predominantly including upper- and upper-middle-class households, were better able to maintain excellent schools and keep crime low, increasing the quality of life while enhancing the value of the voters' largest asset, their houses. Many such jurisdictions have maintained their homogeneous nature by discouraging rental housing, which tends to bring lower income households that might require more social services (especially education) increase crime, and lower prestige.

As mentioned in chapter 1, home mortgage guidelines after World War II mandated racial segregation in the new suburbs. "Redlining" of predominantly black, poor areas in the city became common practice as growth spiraled outward and banks and federal insurance programs refused to support redevelopment or business investment in the cities. The desegregation of public schools mandated in 1954 hastened white flight to the suburbs, leaving city schools to cope with a disproportionately poor student body. The civil rights movement may have been launched with the successful bus boycott in Montgomery, Alabama, but low-income African-Americans ultimately lost the war for better transportation services. As white middle-class riders abandoned bus transit and other public transit systems, the decreasing ridership, political support, and funding meant that there was nominal service to the new suburbs. In many metropolitan areas there was active opposition to the extension of transit to the suburbs to keep minorities from even commuting there. The official desegregation of housing mandated in the 1968 Fair Housing Act allowed blacks and other minority middle-class residents to leave the center cities, just as the majority white population had been doing. This had the ironic result of weakening vibrant black and other minority commercial and housing districts. The race riots of the late 1960s put the final nail in the coffin of many center-city neighborhoods, providing further motivation for most middle-class households, white and minority, to flee the city. The middle class had twin reasons to move out: the positive lure of the drivable sub-urban lifestyle and the negative reaction to declining walkable urban places.

INFLUENCE OF THE FAVORED QUARTER AND SUBURBAN JURISDICTIONS

According to Myron Orfield's *Metropolitics,* the affluent outer-ring suburbs in the favored quarter "dominate regional economic growth and garner a disproportionate share of the region's new roads and other development infrastructure."[11] Orfield also pointed out that much of the funding for this infrastructure is raised from the region as a whole. For example, all car-driving residents in the region pay gas taxes to partially support the building of highways, and taxpayers of the region as a whole pay the rest of the money through their income, property, and sales taxes. This applies to most major infrastructure investments. The unlikely consequence of this pattern of infrastructure development is that the whole region whole pays for infrastructure that tends to be placed in the favored quarter; the poor pay for the infrastructure of the rich. According to Orfield, the central cities of Minneapolis and St. Paul, for example, pay "$6 million a year to help move their middle-class households and businesses to the edge of the region."

An example of this reverse Robin Hood phenomenon is the Illinois Turnpike on the south side of the Chicago metropolitan area. This road has been paid off for years, but still collects tolls. These tolls are used to finance new roads in the northwest favored quarter of the metropolitan area where nearly all new roads have recently been built and where most job growth has gone for years, following the high-end housing. Therefore, the working-class employee living in the poorer, nonfavored quarter in the southern part of the metro area pays tolls to commute to work, which is probably located in the northwest. The tolls help pay for the roads that continue to spread growth to the northwest. Because there is a relationship between the distance from home to work and the value of the house, this worker is subsidizing growth, which both makes the commute longer and lowers the value of his or her home.

One of the few advantages for those still living in the center city was the continued commuting convenience to the remaining downtown jobs coupled with the ability to "reverse commute" if their jobs were in the burgeoning edge cities. Transit, whether rail or bus, would generally work only for jobs in and near downtown, because many transit systems focused on downtown in this era. Transit was generally not a viable option to get to new fringe-located jobs, but if the city dweller had access to a car, the reverse commute was manageable. However, this would not be the case starting in the 1990s in many metro areas, as will be seen in the next chapter.

Certainly the residents of the favored quarter are happy to have the rest of the region help them pay for their infrastructure, but some elements of regional infrastructure are rejected if they are considered a nuisance. For example, the only freeway not built according to the original plan in the Los Angeles region was the Beverly Hills Freeway along Sunset Boulevard. In Phoenix it was the Paradise Valley Freeway. Both would have run right through the heart of the highest-end housing districts in their respective metropolitan areas and the heart of the favored quarter. It is okay to have desirable infrastructure, but freeways that get too close to upper-end neighborhoods are not acceptable. In Atlanta, the building of the Georgia 400 freeway due north of downtown was delayed for many years because it was to go directly through the favored quarter, bisecting the high-end, predominantly white, Buckhead and Dunwoody neighborhoods. Only the leadership of a black Fulton County commissioner got the road built, citing the needs of the black community living on the south side to commute to where the vast majority of new jobs in the metro area were being created in places like Buckhead and Perimeter Center. The commissioner was pictured on the cover of a local business magazine standing in the middle of a road under the headline: "I Will Build This Road," referring to Georgia 400.

The favored quarter is also where "locally undesirable land uses" (LU-LUs) are *not* located. These include dumps, prisons, and homeless shelters. The ultimate LULU is an airport due to the size, traffic, and noise. Of the only two newly sited major airports built in the United States over the past quarter century, both have been located in the opposite direction of the favored quarter. Denver International is located to the northeast, while the favored quarter is to the south. Austin's new airport is located to the east, while the favored quarter is to the northwest.

EDGE CITIES

The employment growth of the 1980s focused on what came to be called "edge cities," a term devised by Joel Garreau in a 1989 book by the same name. "Edge city" was one of about thirty names coined to describe this new metropolitan place, but it was the one that stuck, describing Perimeter

Center (Atlanta), Post Oak (Houston), and Sherman Oaks (Los Angeles), among many others. Edge cities were a new animal where regional-serving functions such as retail, hotels, and offices, came together in a drivable sub-urban manner. These edge cities were where the vast majority of relocating and new jobs concentrated in the 1970s and 1980s. The typical edge city has a regional mall at the major highway intersection, surrounded by surface parking lots. All around the regional mall, like support ships surrounding a mammoth aircraft carrier, are office buildings, other big-box and specialty retail centers, hotels, and possibly a few apartment buildings and condominiums. The streets are four to eight lanes across, and few people ever consider crossing the street on foot; if you are at the mall and want to go to the office building across the street, you get into your car. The area looks exactly like the Futurama model Norman Bel Geddes had created forty years earlier. Futurama had come to life, and a few malls, such as South Coast Plaza in Orange County, California, Somerset Mall I & II in Troy, Michigan, the Galleria Mall in northwest Atlanta, and Tyson's Corner in Virginia just outside of the Washington, D.C., metro area, even had the Futurama elevated walkways.

The new employment concentrating in edge cities quickly grew to be larger than the old central city downtown's employment in most metropolitan areas. Most large and small corporate headquarters and regional offices, many banks, law and accounting firms, and even federal employment centers[12] began a mass exodus to these edge cities in the 1970s and especially in the 1980s. The central city job loss was such that it would have had to increase its annual growth by a factor of two just to maintain its relative market share; many center cities lost jobs in absolute terms. The result was that downtowns, which had more than ninety percent of all occupied office space in the 1950s, saw their market share drop to under forty percent of the region's occupied office space by the end of the 1980s.

The explosion in development in America in the 1980s was unlike that in any other decade in history. More office space was developed during that decade than in all previous American history rolled together. And the vast majority of that office space and the housing, retail, highway, and other infrastructure to support it was in the suburban favored quarter of our metropolitan areas.

By the late-1980s, the cycle was complete; first residential, then retail, and finally jobs left the center city as the domestic policy set up to implement Futurama bore fruit. The mountain had come to Mohamed, and America was a very different place than just thirty years earlier. The 1955 Hill Valley was dead; long live 1985 Hill Valley. The domestic policy and social engineering to implement Futurama had worked.

3

THE STANDARD REAL ESTATE PRODUCT TYPES

Why Every Place Looks Like Every Place Else

The 1980s real estate and infrastructure boom, the largest in American history in terms of the amount built until then, had to come to an end. It was predictably followed in the early 1990s by the worst real estate downturn since the 1930s Depression.

Virtually every product type in real estate—office, industrial, retail, for-sale housing, rental housing, hotel, etc.—saw market demand collapse in the late 1980s, leading to huge vacancy rates and plummeting rental rates and sales prices. Vacancy rates for office space in the early 1990s went well above twenty percent in most markets, sometimes above forty percent. (For comparison, vacancies in a balanced market are between five and eight percent). Sale prices in many formerly hot housing markets, such as California and the Northeast, declined for the first time since the 1930s. As the Homer Hoyt Institute, an independent, non-profit research and educational foundation concerned with real estate, says on its Web site, "During the real estate debacle of the late 1980s and early 1990s, properties lost approximately 30 percent of their value on average, while many properties suffered losses of 50 percent or more.[1] According to standard economics, when the level of economic activity goes down by more than twenty percent, it is officially a depression; the late 1980s and early 1990s were a real estate depression.

The 1980s boom had been financed by banks, insurance companies, and international investors, but most infamously by savings and loans (S&Ls). The partial deregulation of the S&L industry in the early 1980s encouraged these institutions to make risky real estate ventures with minimal fiscal oversight. The S&Ls made these risky, high-yielding loans to counter the still-regulated low-interest mortgage loans on their books. S&Ls were rolling federal government–insured dice—and they lost, which meant that taxpayers and many others lost as well because the deposit insurance bill came due. The result was the collapse of 1,043 S&Ls (one-third of the total), many commercial banks, and a financial hit taken by many real estate institutional investors, including many insurance companies. The entire U.S. banking system was put in jeopardy, so much so that the federal government was forced to take drastic action. As a retrospective Federal Deposit Insurance Corporation (FDIC)–issued study stated, the S&L crisis was "the greatest collapse of US financial institutions since the 1930s."[2]

The S&L financial crisis was *the* defining moment of the past half century for the U.S. real estate industry. This crisis affected the financing of this huge segment of the economy, the budget stability of the federal government, and the overall economic performance of the nation. The bankruptcy of the S&L industry and its consequences marked the end of one era and the beginning of another.

The collapse of these S&Ls and many banks was almost exclusively the result of bad real estate loans. These bad loans were taken over by the federal government, initially through the Federal Savings and Loan Insurance Corporation, then, after a cascade of bad loans made that agency insolvent in 1989, through the FDIC, the insurance provider for commercial banks, which had more financial resources. Many old and respected insurance companies, also holding bad real estate investments and debt in overbuilt real estate markets, took a less well-publicized financial write-down or went bankrupt.

THE FED STEPS IN

The Federal Reserve (aka "the Fed") reacted to this crisis by shutting off most bank and S&L funding of real estate development nationally between 1990 and 1992. Congress set up a bail-out agency, the Resolution Trust Corporation (RTC), in 1989, to assume title to the hundreds of billions of dollars of real estate assets and bad loans from failed S&Ls and banks.

The lending ban on the industry severely limited construction in the country. The Urban Land Institute, a leading real estate think tank, set up the Credit Crunch Task Force to work with the Federal Reserve to lift the ban.

The reaction of the Federal Reserve to the Credit Crunch Task Force, according to Bob Larson, a senior executive with the Wall Street investment banking firm of Lazard Feres & Company, and a member of the task force, was "the Fed told us 'real estate . . . we know the industry is huge but we know very little about it. Put together some economic information about its impact on the economy.'" The Fed was aware neither of the actual size of the real estate industry nor the importance of the industry to the economy—an amazing but true admission. The knowledge gained from this new attention to real estate, such as that it represented about thirty-five percent of the assets of the economy, had wide-ranging implications later, as we shall see.

But first, the RTC engaged in a massive fire sale of the assets the U.S. government had inherited from S&Ls and banks: everything from resort land to office buildings, housing subdivisions to warehouses. Congress injected $124 billion into the U.S. financial system to maintain stability, the equivalent of $207 billion in 2007 dollars,[3] about the same as the federal government spends on transportation, the largest discretionary domestic spending program, over a four-year period.[4] This money was used to make whole depositors in the failed S&Ls and banks who were insured against such a loss by the federally provided deposit insurance. There was considerable criticism that the RTC sold off this real estate too cheaply and that the bailout unjustly penalized taxpayers to offset the scandal-ridden investments caused by the greed of real estate developers and investors.[5] In retrospect, these were some of the best economic decisions ever made.[6] The U.S. economy took a "big bath" of losses related to real estate, but the financial industry's balance sheet stabilized and the economy began to grow once again by 1993. The economy grew during the mid- to late 1990s at a rate not seen since the 1960s; a high-tech-fueled boom was off and running, based on the restored financial base of the country.[7]

THE END OF REAL ESTATE AS WE KNEW IT

Restarting the real estate industry required getting the financial faucet turned back on—allowing banks to lend to the industry again. However, the Federal Reserve needed an oversight mechanism for this huge industry before it would allow lending to resume. No one in the Federal Reserve wanted a repeat of the financial debacle and scandal caused by real estate during the 1980s. The job of oversight was taken over by Wall Street investment banks, the long-time source of investment and debt financing for major corporations, and the managers of the publicly traded financial markets. Wall Street bankers had historically disdained real estate as a locally financed business with somewhat sleazy operators—real estate developers—but they soon learned to love the industry.

A major problem for real estate has always been that it is an illiquid asset class, meaning it was very difficult and time-consuming to buy or sell. In addition, a problem for Wall Street had been that real estate was generally in relatively small ownership pieces. That is, each property was in a separate legal structure, with only the largest assets valued at more than $50 million, which was the smallest asset size that would catch the eye of Wall Street investment bankers in the early 1990s. However, investment bankers got over their hesitancy about real estate by dusting off an old tax category of real estate holding companies, real estate investment trusts (REITs). Each publicly traded REIT owned a bundle of real estate assets, valued in the hundreds of millions of dollars initially, which share-owners could buy and sell on a daily basis through a stock exchange, generally the New York Stock Exchange, providing "liquidity" to real estate ownership for the first time in history.

Investment bankers began a binge of initial public offerings of REITs in 1993. More than eighty new REITs were launched that year, generally consisting of nearly bankrupt real estate portfolios. The developers who owned these bundles of assets were grabbing onto a lifeline by selling their portfolio to the investing public. Wall Street firms also got into the trading of commercial mortgage-backed securities (CMBS) bonds for real estate debt in the early 1990s, a business pioneered by the RTC to get rid of property taken over by the federal government from the bankrupt S&Ls and banks. This new CMBS market came on the heels of Wall Street getting into the secondary residential mortgage business (primary mortgage reselling) in the late 1980s, a market also pioneered by the federal government in the mid-1980s.

By the end of 2005, REITs had a market capitalization of $438 billion, CMBSs were a $721 billion market, and the secondary residential market was $5.5 trillion.[8] Together, these three categories of traded real estate, which did not exist a generation earlier, represented more than three percent of all assets in the country, equal to twenty percent of the asset value of all of the publicly traded companies in the American economy. Wall Street no longer considered real estate chump change. Real estate had become the fourth major financial asset class, joining the three basics: cash, stocks, and bonds.

THE COMMODIFICATION OF THE BUILT ENVIRONMENT

Public markets have a precondition when they agree to trade a company or a product. The public market can only trade "like for like." The market does not want to trade unique things; Wall Street is not an art auction house. Traders want to trade the same kind of thing in high volumes. An oil trader trades defined kinds of oil, such as Louisiana light sweet crude, #2 heating oil, and conventional premium gasoline. All are defined and understood. Stockbrokers want to trade only a defined class of stock, such as class A Intel stock or preferred AT&T stock. No one wants to trade undefined crude oil or special Intel stock; it is too risky and complicated. In other words, public markets trade only items that have been commoditized (made identical). So when Wall Street took on real estate in the form of REITs and CMBSs in the early 1990s, real estate had to commoditize what it built.

The industry did this with what it knew how to build then: drivable sub-urban products. This commoditization resulted in what is referred to as the "nineteen standard real estate product types" that Wall Street knows, understands, and can be traded in large quantities.[9] Any deviation by building a product that was "nonconforming," a term of art on Wall Street, meant that it was not one of the nineteen and that you either did not get financing or, if you did, it was far more expensive.

The real estate industry itself became very specialized. Bank loan officers now specialize in just one of these types of real estate; bring them something different and they will generally show you the door. Conforming real estate products are also much easier to sell; a conforming product type would be attractive to national and international institutional buyers, while nonconforming products are generally of interest only to local and regional buyers, a smaller pool. Wall Street underwriters focus on just one of these product types, knowing all of the developers and owners of that kind of product throughout the country. If a developer asked a Wall Street or a commercial bank underwriter to analyze a different product type or a unique development, he or she would be a fish out of water. It would be like asking a Louisiana sweet crude oil analyst to evaluate the purchase or sale of Intel class A stock.

The nineteen standard product types include entry-level housing subdivisions, suburban garden apartments, warehouses, suburban office

---

BOX 3.1. The Nineteen Standard Real Estate Product Types in 2006[1]

OFFICE

- Build to suit
- Mixed-use urban
- Medical

INDUSTRIAL

- Build to suit
- Warehouse

RETAIL

- Neighborhood center
- Lifestyle center (see chapter 5)
- Big-box anchored

HOTEL

- Business and luxury hotels

APARTMENT

- Suburban garden
- Urban high density

MISCELLANEOUS

- Self storage
- Mobile home park

HOUSING

- Entry level
- Move-up
- Luxury
- Assisted Living/Retirement
- Resort/Second home

---

parks, and others. Developers have been building these standard products over the years, and they have been evolving as drivable sub-urban development patterns unfolded in the pattern shown in chapter 2. There is nothing magical about the exact number nineteen, but the number of market-acceptable product types seems to float around nineteen over time. Box 3.1 outlines the conforming standard product types as of 2006.

EXAMPLES OF THE NINETEEN STANDARD PRODUCT TYPES

An example of a standard product type that most everyone knows is the local-serving neighborhood retail center (figure 3.1), where most Americans buy groceries. As defined by the International Council of Shopping Centers and the Urban Land Institute,[10] the standard neighborhood retail center is on twelve to fifteen acres of land on the going-home side of a four- to eight-lane major arterial road with at least 25,000 cars per day. Its market draw area will have at least 25,000 customers within three miles, preferably with above-average incomes. Twenty percent of the site will be covered by the one-story buildings, which are set back from the street by about 150 feet; the rest of the site will be paved with asphalt for parking in the front and a drive in the rear where deliveries will be made and trash will be hauled away. There will be a 50,000 to 60,000 square foot grocery store with a superior credit rating at one end of the center, and a 20,000 to 25,000 square foot drug store with a superior credit rating at the other end. In between will be the national chains or franchises of all the stores everyone knows and loves, such as "I Can't Believe It's Yogurt," a Hallmark card shoppe, and a Subway sandwich store. During the last fifteen minutes of design, the architect will ask, "Where will this center be located?" If he is told it will be in southern California, a Mediterranean tile roof and stucco will be specified. If it is to be in Washington, D.C., it will have an eighteenth-century Federalist-style brick façade with white pillars.

Like every other of the nineteen standard product types, individual neighborhood retail centers are basically interchangeable. Once a project is judged to be conforming, it can be traded like Monopoly cards, without the acquirer ever going out to look at what is being bought or sold. This is the reason why any suburban place in the country looks pretty much the same as any other. The nineteen standard product types ensure that once you have seen one neighborhood retail center or any other standard product type, you have seen them all. Although this "cookie cutter" style of development was a mark of early drivable sub-urbanism, the commoditization process solidified it into a single nationwide type. The phenomenon was best captured by Tom Wolfe in A Man in Full, when one of the characters is driving through the nameless suburbs of Atlanta and comments, "the only way you could tell you are leaving one community and entering another is when the franchise chains start repeating and

FIGURE 3.1. The neighborhood retail center is the best known standard commercial real estate type, visited often by the 25,000 "neighbors" who shop weekly for their groceries and other day-to-day necessities.

you spotted another 7-Eleven, another Wendy's, another Costco, another Home Depot . . . [T]he new monuments were not office towers or monuments or city halls or libraries or museums but 7-Eleven stores."[11]

The nineteen standard product types have a proven track record of market acceptance and financial performance. They change with the general market conditions throughout the country. For example, in the 1990s developers overbuilt luxury hotels, which temporarily took that product off the list. However, budget hotels during the same time period were in great demand, so they were added to the list. These cheap hotels, such as Motel 6, Baymont Inn, and Days Inn, proliferated in high-traffic-volume, limited-access highway locations, where the product specifications mandated that they be located. The budget motels have since become overbuilt, and in the 2000s, developers are back to building luxury and business hotels, following the recovery of the high-end travel market after September 11, 2001, so luxury and business hotels are once again a standard product type. The overbuilding of budget hotels has not been worked through, so they are off the list for now.

Some of the other standard product types in 2006 are described below.

■ **LUXURY FOR-SALE HOUSING**—This product will almost always be located in the favored quarter, preferably in a guarded, gated community. Luxury for-sale housing will include almost every amenity within the home (home entertainment room, indoor pool/Jacuzzi, exercise room, etc.). Often the community will include a golf course and a lavish clubhouse. The development may sell both finished lots for custom-built houses and speculative houses for those who want a home immediately. The finishes on the houses will be the highest level, although the basic construction will generally still be stick-built with sheetrock walls, with the narrowly defined "must-have" brand-name appliances (e.g., Sub Zero refrigerators, Wolfe cooktops and stoves, Bosch dishwashers, Asko clothes washers and dryers) that proclaim that the house is top-drawer. The municipality in which the project is located will have excellent public schools, though they will likely not be required, because most households will consist of empty-nesters with no school-age children living in the home or the children will be sent to private schools no matter how good the public schools are. The socioeconomic "target market" is closely managed to make sure that only those with a defined high income level are admitted. Housing aimed at "lower" income households, those making less than $200,000 per year, will definitely be avoided at all costs. Only those that are "just like us," known as JLUs in the jargon, will be allowed.

■ **MOVE-UP FOR-SALE HOUSING**—This housing will also be in the favored quarter, though is less likely to be in a gated community. This type includes so-called "McMansions" and other oversized homes that provide "value." Although large, these houses are not especially well built (hollow doors, sheetrock walls, and midlevel appliances). Yet on a price-per-square-foot basis, they are very reasonably priced. The "curb appeal" of these homes is extremely important; they must look as large and impressive from the street as possible. The development will be located in a good public school system. When initially purchasing a new home, there will be a few models to tour, and possibly some speculative homes for immediate purchase, but most will be built to order with a reasonable range of options available for upgrades.

■ **ENTRY-LEVEL FOR-SALE HOUSING**—This type of housing will probably be located outside the favored quarter, particularly if the target buyers will be minorities. The homes will be extremely cheaply built with many synthetic materials (plywood, vinyl siding, etc.) and factory-made components (joists, stairs, showers, etc.) that are assembled on-site rather than built on-site. Depending on the strength of the market, speculative homes may be available for immediate purchase or can be ordered for future delivery. There will be a model complex of three to four houses inside a "trap," that is, a fence surrounding all of the models to keep the shoppers in the model complex once they enter. If the homes are ordered for construction and purchase, there will be a "design center," probably in the garage of one of the models if it is on-site, or the design center may be off-site, generally visible from a freeway serving many subdivisions for the home-building company. The design center will offer options for finishes in the house, such as different flooring options (wall-to-wall, tile, wood, etc.), different counter options (Formica, Corian, etc.), different cabinet options (medium density fiberboard, known as MDF, wood laminate, etc.), among other features. The concept is to sell as many "upgrades" as possible, because these are extremely profitable items, similar to options on a car. The homebuilder will also try to have buyers use their own mortgage company, a very profitable service, which allows the home builder to control the financing process. Every visitor will be tracked carefully following the visit with continual sales and market research follow-up to better understand whom the sub-division is attracting and the effectiveness of their marketing and advertising campaign.

■ **GARDEN RENTAL APARTMENTS**—These are two- to three-story drivable sub-urban apartments (figure 3.2) known as "walk-ups," because there is generally no elevator. These will be either "flats" or townhouses or some combination of the two. During the 1990s, individual garages were introduced

FIGURE 3.2. The standard garden, or walk-up, apartment complex contains at least 150 units and fronts a busy street from which most of the potential customers initially see it as they are driving by. (Source: The Springs 650 Ebbcreek Dr., Corona, CA. Managed by Avalon Communities. Constructed 1987. Number of apartments: 320)

into many of the new complexes being built, though plenty of surface parking was included for residents and guests. These complexes will typically include more than 150 units and often many more to allow for economies of scale for marketing, amenities, and management. There will be a pool, Jacuzzi, exercise room, and maybe a business center. Management will be provided 24/7. The construction quality will be rather cheap, akin to entry-level for-sale housing. The location will be on a major arterial highway or freeway with maximum visibility from passing cars; more than seventy percent of new tenants will find out about the apartment complex from driving by.

■ **BUILD-TO-SUIT INDUSTRIAL OR OFFICE**—The build-to-suit product (figure 3.3) is actually a development process. It generally starts with a developer who owns highway-accessible and possibly highway-visible land that

FIGURE 3.3. This 2-million-square-foot, build-to-suit, research and development building, the GMC Truck Product Center of General Motors, was completed by Etkin Equities, LLC, in Pontiac, Michigan, in 1998. It is twenty-eight miles from downtown Detroit in the middle of the favored quarter, typical of the location of large corporate build-to-suit development during the 1990s and 2000s. (Source: Centerpoint Business Campus—A Development of Etkin Equities)

is properly zoned for industrial/warehouse or office use. Build-to-suit is the building block of the "edgeless city," which will be discussed shortly. The corporate user will negotiate with the landowner/developer for the kind of building required (e.g., type of construction, size, loading docks, parking spaces, tenant improvements, lease or own, lease terms, etc.). If it is a building that the user wants to own, a price will be determined. If it is a lease, the most important issues are how long the lease will be and the creditworthiness of the tenant. The developer will rely on the sales contract or lease to obtain financing. The lease will typically be for twenty years, the length of the typical "take-out" loan, comparable to a house mortgage. Matching the length of the lease with the loan is the ideal situation. Any building life left after the lease expires is considered gravy—nice but not expected. The building can always be torn down and the land recycled for the next potential use.

KEEPING DEVELOPERS ON A SHORT LEASH

Because low-density, drivable sub-urban products became the basis of what Wall Street could finance, and Wall Street was new to real estate finance, there has been great hesitancy to broaden the list of conforming products. With a few exceptions, Wall Street and institutional investors tended not to finance mixed-use, complex, walkable urbanism as of 2006. Wall Street bankers also wanted to keep real estate developers, not known for their conservatism,[12] on a short leash. If REIT executives got into a mixed-use development project, the Wall Street analysts would warn them in no uncertain terms that they should "stick to their knitting" unless they wanted to be downgraded to a "sell" recommendation.

The specialization of the industry and the need to bow to Wall Street's wishes are clear in the story of a chief executive officer (CEO) of a major regional mall REIT. In 2002, I asked him to consider building a mixed-use walkable housing and retail project immediately adjacent to the company's flagship mall in Tennessee. He declined to even consider it because his company had just been criticized in a front-page Wall Street Journal story for engaging in general contracting to build their own regional malls, rather than hiring an independent company. Being in the regional mall building *contracting* business was seen as being a diversion to *developing and managing* them. Getting into the Main Street retail and housing business could have made the investment community call for his firing and a downgrade in the rating of the company's stock.

Two REITs went public in 1993 with a mission of developing mixed-use walkable projects: Post Properties, an apartment developer, and Federal Realty, a retail developer. The two would occasionally pursue joint ventures together, with Federal Realty doing the retail on the ground floor and Post Properties doing the apartments on top. After a few years, Wall Street came to the conclusion that this strategy was too unusual and strongly urged the boards of both companies to change to conforming products. Their CEOs, who were both the founders of the companies, were fired, and the company strategies shifted to the building of only standard drivable sub-urban products.

It does seem strange that Wall Street investment bankers have a hard time financing walkable urbanism. At the end of the workday, most of them leave their office building in downtown or midtown Manhattan, which is probably among the most expensive in the world, and walk home past shops that pay the most rent on the planet to their $1,000- to $2,500-per-square-foot loft, condominium, or townhouse, again, some of the most pricey in the country. They are living, working, and shopping in some of the best and, not coincidentally, most expensive walkable urbanism in the country.

EDGELESS CITIES

Once funding for real estate became available again around 1993, much of the growth went even farther out to the fringe, leaping beyond edge cities (described in chapter 2) to what Dr. Robert Lang of Virginia Tech called "edgeless cities."[13] In the 1990s, drivable sub-urbanism was on steroids. The only unifying element was the limited-access highway that connected work and home. Edgeless cities that were beyond the beyond emerged as southern Oklahoma became a suburb of Dallas and eastern West Virginia became a suburb of Washington, D.C. There were no centers in this new kind of sprawl, there was no "place," there was no "there there." Growth was an amorphous blob pushing out where no man had gone before.

As the real estate industry recovered from the crushing early-1990s depression, there were few developers to build anything; they were basically bankrupt and scrambling for the new financing Wall Street had just created. The famous developer Sam Zell coined the motto in 1991 that proved prescient for the real estate industry, "stay alive until '95." Without developers to build, corporations led the way to the fringe, building new offices, factories, and warehouses on limited-access highways just beyond the former edge of the metropolitan area, constructing build-to-suit or "owner-occupied" buildings. No one knows how many jobs were moved or created in these formless, edgeless cities. Records are not kept about how many square feet of new owner-occupied buildings are constructed.

FIGURE 3.4. The Sears Holding Company headquarters, the result of the merger of Sears into the acquiring Kmart Corporation in 2004, is thirty-seven miles from downtown Chicago in what is now referred to as an edgeless city. (Source: Courtesy of Sears, Roebuck and Co.)

This is because very little or none of this new development is leased on the open market. When industrial, retail, or office space is leased to third-party tenants, it is listed by the major commercial brokerage firms such as CB/Richard Ellis or Grubb & Ellis and data are collected by third-party firms such as Black's Guide or Co-Star. Because much of the new space built in the 1990s and early 2000s was owner-occupied or built to suit, there was no reason for any organization, public or private, to collect data about its existence.

Billions of square feet of commercial, retail, and industrial real estate product were built in the 1990s and early 2000s and millions of jobs were relocated or created and no one—not the U.S. Census, U.S. Department of Agriculture, which tracks land-use conversion, or real estate trade associations—knows how much and where exactly it went. Driving thirty-seven miles northwest of downtown Chicago to the 2-million-square-foot Sears headquarters (figure 3.4) (where on a clear day you can see their former 110-story downtown headquarters, which is also 2 million square feet) or twenty miles south of Kansas City to the 2-million-square-foot Sprint world headquarters, one can see that much of the owner-user development went out to the absolute fringe (though it is still in the favored quarter). It's just that no one has bothered to count it.

The rise of large owner-user office and industrial complexes on the edgeless city fringe showed that another phase of metropolitan growth was underway. In essence, the bosses making these decisions chose to avoid traffic congestion by going against traffic during rush hour. In addition, the proliferation of big-box centers occurred in the 1990s, led by Wal-Mart, Target, Sam's Club, and Costco, and the fringe was the easiest place to find large amounts of land to build their "super centers" or locate new power centers.

Home builders began developing again by the mid-1990s as they obtained financing and began to follow the commercial and industrial plants out to the fringe and beyond. Figure 3.5 shows these new development patterns, which built upon the patterns of the previous decades shown in figure 2.1, but the map has to be presented at a different scale, because most metropolitan areas mushroomed in size in the 1990s. For every one percent population growth in the 1990s and early 2000s, land use grew by probably ten to twenty percent, even faster geometric land use consumption than in the 1970s and 1980s.[14]

The country viewed from this perspective seemed like it would never stop sprawling to an ever-expanding fringe. What were once called edge cities in the 1980s were twenty to thirty miles inside the new edge of the metropolitan area by 2006, where they are now locations for redevelopment and in-fill. The 1980s term "edge city" lost its meaning. New York City and Philadelphia, Boston and Providence, and Washington, D.C. and Baltimore were all growing together. An urban center dubbed "Chattlanta" spread across northern Georgia and southern Tennessee. Greater Los Angeles had become 5,000 square miles in size, as large as the state of Connecticut.

It seemed at the end of the 1980s that the pendulum simply couldn't swing any further toward drivable sub-urbanism, but it did, now with the

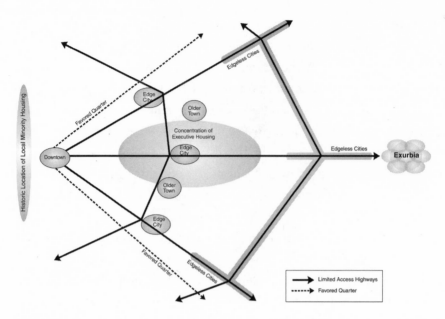

FIGURE 3.5. By the middle of the first decade of the twenty-first century, nearly all metropolitan areas had expanded even faster and farther than during the 1980s, as shown in figure 2.1. The 1980s metro area edge cities and limited access highways are still there, but growth has continued farther into the favored quarter to edgeless cities and exurbia along new or expanded limited-access highways. For every one percent population growth, the physical size of American metro areas increased by probably ten to twenty percent.

financial power of Wall Street behind it. The spread continues, despite the increasingly apparent negative consequences of building this one development form to the exclusion of all others. Yet as we shall see, a countertrend was brewing—one that could fundamentally transform real estate, how we invest thirty-five percent of our wealth, and the way Americans live.

4

CONSEQUENCES OF DRIVABLE SUB-URBAN GROWTH

When the Futurama social experiment began to change the built environment after World War II, there were no historical precedents. There was little we could learn from the previous 5,500 years of building cities, because the lessons of walkable urbanism did not apply to drivable sub-urban development. We were making it up as we went along. Though there was some experimentation with drivable sub-urbanism in the 1920s, generally the building of cities in the decades and centuries prior to the Depression versus after 1945, when the country started building drivable sub-urban metropolitan areas, was as different as night and day.

Few real estate developers who had built homes, offices, and retail prior to the Depression were still in business in the late 1940s. It seemed as if the entire real estate industry got collective amnesia about how to construct the built environment. A *New Yorker* cartoon from late 1943 showed a business owner saying to a colleague, "Now what did we make before we got all these government contracts?" Meanwhile, the Futurama seed grew in the American consciousness; its car-based transportation system would drive us in an entirely different and new direction.

We now understand various things about the consequences of drivable sub-urban growth—intended and unintended, positive and negative.

Like many things in life, the good news is that we successfully implemented the Futurama-inspired vision of the future; the bad news is that we successfully implemented the Futurama-inspired vision of the future.

POSITIVE CONSEQUENCES OF DRIVABLE SUB-URBANISM

Perhaps the most straightforward positive consequence of drivable sub-urban residential development is delivering on its Jeffersonian promise to provide what could be called "terrestrial affiliation,"[1] having a piece of dirt to call one's own. The cramped urban dweller or the transplanted farmer generally yearned for a garden or yard. Drivable sub-urbanism allowed this for almost everyone.

Another major benefit of drivable sub-urban development is that it is cheaper to build for a number of reasons. The typical low-density American house uses wood-frame construction, which is about the least expensive construction system available, cheaper than steel frame, concrete, and even adobe. Because commercial drivable sub-urbanism, such as a strip mall, is normally set back from the street, its "billboard architecture" is trying to catch drivers' attention as they go by at forty-five miles per hour. It does just fine with cheaper construction and synthetic finishes, because at those speeds and distance, no one can easily ascertain architectural and construction quality.

Development financing has also encouraged cheaper construction, particularly for commercial projects that produce a cash flow (as opposed to for-sale housing). The bottom line is that in contemporary finance used by the United States and other advanced nations, it is critical to get a return on the investor's money as quickly as possible. The best means of doing this is to reduce construction costs to minimize the required upfront investment. Since drivable sub-urbanism became the unofficial U.S. domestic policy sixty years ago, real estate has changed from a long-term asset, generally an investment that has ongoing value for upward of forty years, to a short- to mid-term asset class. Today, a commercial real estate investment has a seven- to ten-year lifespan before a major renovation is required, it is left to degrade, or it is bulldozed. Modern offices rarely have the construction quality of pre-1930 buildings, in spite of technological advances. The wood frames of contemporary entry- and middle-level housing are generally not strong enough to be self-supporting—the sheetrock interior walls literally give them their structural integrity. There are obvious short-term cost benefits to consumers in this cheaper construction, but the end result is that modern construction quality is generally considered much worse than almost anything built prior to the 1930s Depression.[2] There is an obvious irony in this; today's Americans make three times more in real dollar terms than our ancestors living in the 1920s, yet we can not seem to build buildings of as high quality as those built then.[3]

Drivable sub-urban for-sale housing development also results in cheaper land costs per dwelling unit if the consumer is willing to "drive until you qualify." Various studies have shown that for every mile from an employment center a home buyer is willing to drive, the price of the house drops by between 1.5 and 6.0 percent.[4] Housing affordability has therefore been directly tied to transportation. "Drive until you qualify" has become the basic American affordable housing policy.

Smaller suburban governments allow households to cluster together in relatively homogeneous jurisdictions—the "birds of a feather flock together" phenomenon described in chapter 2. Sociologists have found that this flocking together of people "just like us" (JLUs) is crucial to the selection of a neighborhood in which to live, raise, and educate children, and invest in the largest family asset. This self-segregation is part of what seems to drive us all. Drivable sub-urbanism allowed birds of a feather to live together in small, separate political jurisdictions to an extent not possible before.

These smaller, homogeneous suburban governments are able to avoid many of the expenses associated with having lower income residents, who tend to need costly government services. Lower income residents have been discouraged from joining these communities through minimum-lot-size regulations, restrictions on the building of rental apartment complexes, and bans on "granny flats" that might attract renters, among other methods.

These smaller jurisdictions populated by JLUs tend to have a higher tax base, which results in better funded public schools. One of the most important factors for families with children in selecting a home is, of course, the quality of the public schools. The average SAT and ACT scores of every school district in the nation are now available online, and this information directly affects housing prices.

One of the most important unintended positive consequences of drivable sub-urbanism is increased privacy. By embracing drivable sub-urbanism, Americans have achieved a level of privacy unknown in history. According to Janna Smith in her book, *Privacy Matters,* "The amount of privacy possible in suburbia is historically remarkable."[5] This particularly applies to the time spent by oneself in the car, where you can sing along with the radio, apply makeup, or let off steam. Privacy can also include having the house to oneself or even living alone, something not allowed for women according to the laws of some U.S. states in the eighteenth century. To the 1939 working- or middle-class person living in cramped quarters and riding through Futurama, this kind of privacy seemed almost unimaginable.

There is also a perception that the drivable sub-urban communities are safer than walkable urban places. This perception has become part of the consciousness of the country. I present some evidence below showing that this may not be true.

Last and most definitely not least, a big benefit of drivable urbanism is abundant free parking. Having a place to easily stash the car amid daily errands is critical in drivable sub-urbia, and it is something that is now expected. The planning for drivable sub-urban development starts with the parking potential of a piece of land, and *then* the building is designed. For commercial development, the planning almost always means that the parking solution is an at-grade surface lot in front of the building. The building is set back from the street, so anyone driving by can see that there is plenty of parking available. Zoning codes often require enough parking for the times of its heaviest use. According to Donald Shoup, author of *The High Cost of Free Parking,* parking policies are responsible for much of the look of development today.[6]

In summary, the benefits of drivable sub-urbanism have come down to:

- terrestrial affiliation—having a piece of land to call one's own,
- lower costs, due to inherently cheaper construction and infrastructure subsidies,
- more land, particularly if one is willing to "drive until you qualify,"
- lower community taxes,
- improved public schools,
- privacy,
- perceived safety, and
- abundant free parking.

Getting better services, privacy, and more house for a lower cost is about as good as it gets. The domestic policy of promoting drivable sub-urbanism made the decision what could only be called a "no-brainer." What's not to like?

UNINTENDED NEGATIVE CONSEQUENCES OF DRIVABLE SUB-URBANISM

However, there is no such thing as a free lunch; there are always unintended, generally negative, consequences to any social engineering experiment. Aside from obvious racist restrictions imposed by federal, state, and local regulations (voided by late 1940s) and private covenants, conditions, and restrictions (voided by 1970), there was no conspiracy. The domestic policy of the country was attempting to promote a certain way of living, and we got what we subsidized, zoned, and financed, and what the transportation system we selected allowed to be built—to the exclusion of everything else. These unintended consequences are many times the flip side of the benefits most people received as a result of drivable sub-urban development.

Auto Dependence

As mentioned earlier, the selection of a car-based transportation system drove out most other transportation options, such as public transit, bicycles, and especially walking, and this automobile dependence is at the root of many of the negative consequences detailed below.

Initially, two key selling points of the interstate highway program were that it would be user-funded, through federal gas taxes, and that it would provide transportation flexibility. The system was sold as being entirely paid for by user taxes. This did not turn out to be true. Only fifty-six percent of the capital and operating costs for the highway system has been paid for by the gas tax or tolls; the remaining forty-four percent is made up by general tax dollars.[7] Drivable sub-urbanism has also required never-ending investments in more road infrastructure; more than 2 million additional miles of local and collector roads will be needed by 2025 if drivable sub-urban growth continues unchecked.[8]

The second selling point, transportation flexibility, also turned out not to be true. As discussed in chapter 2, a car-based transportation system *decreases* transportation flexibility. Although automobiles provide unprecedented mobility and the lure of the open road, this decentralized transportation system in many cases allows only cars to connect work to home, home to shopping, and home to school. Distances are too great to support convenient transit service and generally make walking impractical.

Traffic congestion is now such an issue that people build their lives around avoiding it and major urban areas offer traffic updates around the clock via radio and the Internet. But for many drivers, sitting in traffic is the only viable option. Ironically, the automobile-based transportation system is turning out to be far less flexible than promised.

Social Segregation

CONCENTRATION OF POVERTY. Recent research by Alan Berube and Bruce Katz at The Brookings Institution showed that concentrated poverty (defined as a census tract with more than twenty percent of the households living below the poverty line) has been increasing since the 1950s. This has resulted in "reduced private sector investment and local job opportunities, increased prices for the poor, higher levels of crime, negative impacts on mental and physical health; low quality neighborhood schools; and heavy burdens on local governments that induce outmigration of middle-class households."[9] Concentrated poverty increases social problems and makes it exceedingly difficult for most people trapped within to break out of its downward spiral. The ability of the middle class, and especially the upper-middle-class, to segregate themselves over the past half century of drivable sub-urbanism, leaving behind areas of increased concentrations of poverty, explains much of the crime, violence, and dead-end lives in U.S. society.

LACK OF ACCESS TO JOBS. In the 1990s and the 2000s as jobs moved out to even more distant edge cities of the favored quarter, twelve to thirty miles and more from the center city, with poor or no transit connections, these jobs were not commutable for most low-income residents, and even moderate-income housing was often not available nearby. This resulted in a severe housing/jobs imbalance in which the unemployment rate on the fringe of the favored quarter was at or below theoretical full employment (less than four percent) while it was twice that amount on the other side of the metropolitan area. The jobs that went begging were virtually impossible to commute to even with a readily available and affordable car.

EXCLUSION OF NONDRIVERS FROM SOCIETY. One minority class has been excluded from "normal" participation in society. These people can participate only if the majority agrees to assist them. They are the nondrivers. At least thirty-three percent of Americans (about 100 million) do not drive; they are too old, too young, too poor, disabled, or not interested.[10, 11] The everyday consequences of this status are evident by the high unemployment rates in the minority housing districts of our central cities and non-favored-quarter inner suburbs. The consequences of not being able to drive were shown dramatically during the evacuation of New Orleans following the collapse of the levees after Hurricane Katrina.

Nondriver status also figures everyday in the proverbial "soccer mom" having to chauffer children or others around town between school, organized sports, other lessons, and home. That many children have to rely upon their parents for everything they do beyond their yard until they obtain their driver's license at age sixteen (which results in an even more grave safety problem, as noted below) results in a disturbing drop in physical activity, a rise in childhood obesity, a vast increase in drug-based treatments for hyperactivity and depression, and a lack of social skills with which to maneuver in the world on their own. Is it any surprise that given the nearly exclusive reliance on drivable sub-urban development, where the *only* way to get around is by car, and bike riding, walking, and transit are infeasible, that children have to be medicated?

SECESSION OF THE ELITES. Flocking together of birds of a feather is inevitable for most socioeconomic groups, but it is a hallmark of drivable sub-urbanism. There is no law against it, and it should be allowed. However, the well-to-do households earning in the top five percent seem to be increasingly seceding from society. Because they've moved to small suburban jurisdictions, gated communities, and second-home/resort locations, the top income earners appear to be less involved in public schools and local government services, such as parks and police protection. Instead they seem to be relying on private providers more heavily, such as private schools, their own clubs, and private guards for formerly publicly provided needs. I believe that as a result it is likely that higher income households will be less willing to fund capital projects and services for the common good, though this has not been documented. The late conservative philosopher Christopher Lasch referred to this as "the revolt of the elite," as "a two-class society in which the favored few monopolize the advantages of money, education, and power." Lasch felt that "the talented retain many of the vices of aristocracy without its virtues . . . [they lack] any acknowledgment of reciprocal obligations between the favored few and the multitude."[12]

NIMBY NEIGHBORHOOD GROUPS. Although participation in volunteer activities and voting has been in decline for decades,[13] one of the fastest growing social phenomena has been the rise of community associations and neighborhood groups. Prior to 1960, there were parent-teacher associations, bowling leagues, fraternal organizations, and religious institutions, but relatively few neighborhood groups. Community associations and neighborhood groups have grown substantially in this country in the last forty years. In 1970, there were 10,000 communities associations representing one percent of the population of the country. By 2006, there were 286,000 community associations representing nineteen percent of the population.[14] These estimates are undoubtedly conservative, because many informal neighborhood groups are not included in these numbers. Today it seems that most neighborhoods have some form of neighborhood organization to track threats to the area from developers, lobby elected officials for infrastructure improvements, demand government services, manage common infrastructure, and attempt to influence renovations and changes by homeowners and commercial businesses that are viewed as not in keeping with the character of the area.

Many neighborhood groups now have formal governmental standing regarding their involvement in new development in their area. Albuquerque, New Mexico, and Washington, D.C., both have given neighborhood groups official input into local development and zoning changes. Much of this input tends to be negative and has led to the acronym NIMBY—not in my backyard. The groups are generally, though not always, opposed to change. Their generally negative reaction to most development is perfectly rational in most drivable sub-urban locations because new growth generally does destroy or reduce the very qualities that brought people to the suburbs in the first place.

Environmental Effects

LAND CONSUMPTION. Drivable sub-urban development has lead to the unprecedented geometric increase in the amount of land being developed for every new resident, as initially mentioned in chapters 2 and 3. According to the U.S. Department of Agriculture (USDA) and U.S. Census, metropolitan land use in the latter half of the twentieth century outpaced by at least *four times* the rate of metropolitan population growth, as we relocated farther and farther from the center to an ever-expanding fringe.[15] In all probability, the land consumption in the last two decades of the twentieth century was actually at least *six to eight times* faster than metropolitan population growth, because the USDA does not consider some of the lowest density development popular over the past generation, such as McMansions on two-acre lots,[16] as urban land use. A 2006 Brookings Institution study focused on "exurbia," the fringe of a metropolitan area that is also not considered urbanized by the USDA, found even more extreme land consumption.[17] Completely car-dependent, exurbia has on average fourteen acres of land for every house (compared to 0.8 acres per house for the typical new suburb), meaning that if exurban land consumption is also considered, there has been a far more rapid geometric increase of ten to twenty times faster than population growth during the last two decades of the twentieth century. Although eighty-three percent of the country's population is located in metropolitan areas, another six percent (10.8 million people) is in exurbia, and this exurban population is growing at more than twice the national population rate, as shown in the Brookings Institution report.[18]

Once land is converted from farm or wilderness to drivable sub-urbanism, it almost never returns. Some of the nation's fastest growing metropolitan areas are projected to consume as much as sixty percent of their nonfederal natural lands over the next twenty-five years.[19] More than 2.2 million acres of farmland, forests, and wetlands are lost to development every year in the United States.[20] About half of that loss is farms; a majority of U.S. fruit, vegetable, and dairy farming takes place very close to urban areas, but productivity of these farms is threatened by encroaching development and new suburban neighbors who object to the smells, sights, and sounds of nearby active farms.[21]

The forests, fields, and wetlands consumed by drivable sub-urbanism leave fewer places for wild plants and animals to live, and fewer safe corridors for migrating birds and animals. The situation is dire for endangered species, sixty percent of which are found in metropolitan areas; almost thirty percent live in rapidly growing metro areas.[22] Already, thirty percent of the plant and animal species in the United States are at risk of disappearing.[23]

HEAT ISLANDS. Replacing stands of trees with pavement and one-story buildings is a hallmark of drivable sub-urban development, and this phenomenon has an immediate impact on metropolitan areas through the creation of heat islands. The loss of the cooling function of trees, combined with the increase in pavement and roofs, contributes to a regional heat island, raising the temperature across the region, increasing air-conditioning demand, worsening smog, and resulting in more heat-related illnesses.[24]

WATER QUALITY. The pavement and buildings of drivable sub-urban development cover a lot of ground, and that impervious surface keeps rainwater from soaking into the soil. Instead, rainwater runs across the pavement, picking up trash, oil, and grease, and flows into storm drains, to be dumped directly into streams. A U.S. Environmental Protection Agency analysis comparing runoff from a subdivision of eight houses on one-acre lots to eight houses on quarter-acre lots found that the large-lot subdivision generated more than 18,000 cubic feet of polluted runoff per year, three times the runoff from the more compact development. The surge in runoff results in more flooding as well.[25]

AIR QUALITY. Everyone knows automobiles are a big contributing factor to many types of air pollution, including soot and the compounds that create ozone. Public policy has focused on reducing tailpipe emissions. However, research shows that the way communities are built has a big impact on how much people drive, and that affects air pollution levels.

The amount that Americans drive—measured as "vehicle miles traveled" (VMT)—increased by 226 percent between 1983 and 2001, despite population growth of just twenty-two percent during that time period.[26]

The geometric growth in VMT is partially attributable to changing demographics and increased wealth, but sixty-four percent of the growth is attributable to land-use changes that have increased trip distances and increased the number of trips made.[27] Many studies have documented that drivable sub-urbanism is linked to longer trips and more miles driven.[28]

Although tailpipe cleanups have been successful in improving air quality, the increase in driving has offset those gains,[29] and many metropolitan areas continue to struggle with meeting the air quality standards set in the Clean Air Act.

CLIMATE CHANGE. Virtually no reasonable person now doubts that the climate is warming and, backed up by overwhelming scientific evidence from the 2007 United Nations Intergovernmental Panel on Climate Change report, most people understand that climate change is occurring largely due to the actions of humans (ninety percent probability).[30] The major cause is the release of carbon dioxide and other gases that trap heat, causing the greenhouse effect. The United States is the largest producer of greenhouse gases on the planet, accounting for twenty-five percent of total emissions. Transportation, primarily the burning of gasoline by cars and trucks, accounts for thirty-three percent of greenhouse gas emissions in the United States.[31] Commercial (office and retail) and residential buildings are responsible for thirty-nine percent of greenhouse gas emissions in this country; the majority of these emissions result from electricity generation through coal-burning power plants. So the commercial/residential built environment and transportation directly result in seventy-two percent of the country's contribution to greenhouse gas emissions; the rest comes from fixed point emissions such as industrial plants.[32] The contribution of drivable sub-urban development to greenhouse gas emissions has not been measured, though this research is underway at The Brookings Institution, among other research centers. However, a study in Atlanta by Dr. Lawrence Frank, of the University of British Columbia, found that "the travel patterns of residents of the least walkable neighborhoods result in about twenty percent higher carbon dioxide emissions than travel by those who live in the most walkable neighborhoods."[33] William Rees, the developer of the "ecological footprint" concept, estimates that a family living in a large-lot single-family home uses about two-thirds more energy than a family living in a more compact, high-density environment.[34] So it is safe to say that low-density development is probably a significant, if not yet well defined, contributor to greenhouse gas emissions.

Much recent attention to solutions to climate change has focused on improving the technical performance of automobiles and buildings. Many hold out great hope for zero-emission vehicles.

The U.S. Green Building Council has created LEED (Leadership in Energy and Environmental Design) building standards, certification, and training that are facilitating a nascent boom in green building. However, less attention has been paid to patterns of land use dictated by drivable sub-urbanism, though the LEED-ND (Neighborhood Development) standards are beginning to address this. These standards are in the pilot stage and are designed to more carefully consider location and transportation issues in green building standards. To reduce greenhouse gas emissions, it is probably best to follow the advice given by Mr. Miyagi in the "immortal" movie, *Karate Kid:* "the best defense is not to be there." The best way to avoid car and truck emissions is to avoid nearly exclusive reliance upon cars and trucks for transportation by building more compact, energy-efficient places.

Health Implications

Many of the negative consequences of drivable sub-urbanism affect health; for example, air pollution contributes to respiratory disease, is associated with an increase in death rates, and appears to make children more susceptible to asthma.[35] Recent research by Dr. Lawrence Frank has found that drivable sub-urbanism is a significant contributor to higher rates of obesity.[36] This is intuitive because many activities that we once did on foot or bicycle, such as going to school or getting groceries from a neighborhood store, and even the tradition of bicycle-riding newspaper boys, are now overwhelming taken care of from behind the wheel of a car. A recent study by Dr. Frank found that for every additional half hour per week residents of the Atlanta metropolitan area drove, they were three percent more likely to be obese.[37] Physical inactivity is associated not just with obesity, but with a host of diseases and conditions, including diabetes, heart disease, and some cancers. A recent study comparing the health of people in more and less sprawling locations found that very spread-out places had about 100 more health problems per 1,000 people than areas that were less sprawling.[38] A number of other studies have found that places that are the opposite of drivable sub-urbanism—with a mix of different uses, higher density, and more connected street networks—inspire more walking and bicycling, and better health.[39]

Drivable sub-urbanism results in triple the rate of severe traffic injuries and death versus walkable urbanism.[40] This results simply from the increased amount of time spent sitting in a car, which exposes the occupants to greater risk of a car accident. Researcher William Lucy at the University of Virginia has found that the safety from crime gained by living in suburban jurisdictions is offset by the greater chance of being killed in a car accident—making the death rate from traffic crashes and homicide higher in some suburban counties than in central cities.[41] Cars are infinitely more safe from a design and construction perspective than thirty years ago, but they are driven so much more that much of the safety gains are offset: the number of Americans killed in car crashes annually has remained stubbornly close to 40,000 for years.[42] This situation is just the opposite of what drivable sub-urbanism promised and what most people still think is reality today. This is particularly ironic because many people believe that drivable sub-urban places are the safest places to raise children, but they may be as dangerous as the cities many families left behind.

The increased traffic means huge new roads and widening of existing roads. Two-lane roads in a walkable urban place, such as the Main Streets of old, act as a unifier of the community. In a drivable sub-urban place, the four- to eight-lane roads become the dividers of the community. To cross these multilane commercial roads is to risk your life. Suburban families no longer let their children cross these huge streets, so many children have no choice but to be bussed to school and driven for extracurricular activities and even to visit friends, even if the distance "as the crow flies" is small. One of the most outspoken critics of suburban development, James Howard Kunstler, referred to these huge roads as "traffic sewers," which most neighborhood activists would find an apt description.

In addition to the threats to physical health, the emotional toll of drivable sub-urbanism is gaining greater attention. Richard Louv, a journalist who has written extensively about the connection between drivable sub-urban development patterns and children's social, physical, and emotional health, reports: "In a typical week, only six percent of children ages nine to thirteen play outside on their own. Even riding a bike is down by thirty-one percent since 1995."[43]

Economic Effects

PERSONAL FINANCES. Although drivable sub-urbanism has resulted in lower housing costs, the real price of these houses is hidden in the gas tank. Transportation costs were eighteen percent of household income in 2005, second to the amount U.S. families spent on housing (twenty-four percent).[44] This compares to fourteen percent spent on transportation by the average family in Europe, where public transit is much more developed and there is more walkable urbanism.[45] The geometric increase in VMT, cited above, also indicates the increasing share that automobile transportation plays in U.S. family finances. AAA calculated that the average cost of car ownership and maintenance for a typical car in 2006 was $7,800 per year.[46] This covers loan payments, fuel, parking, maintenance, insurance, and incidental costs. This $7,800 item in the family budget is paid for in *after-tax* dollars, which means that if the household's combined state and federal tax bracket is twenty percent, the family would have to earn $9,750 in *pretax* salary to pay for each car ($7,800 divided by eighty percent). The result is that owning an average car is the equivalent of having an additional $135,000 mortgage (mortgage interest is tax-deductible, and this calculation assumes six percent mortgage interest). In essence, drivable sub-urbanism has probably been shifting family spending away from investing in a long-term *appreciating* asset (e.g., a house) or savings to a short-term *depreciating* asset (e.g., a car).

The above calculations were for a typical car-owning family, but the findings become even more grim for a working-class family. A 2006 study of eighteen metropolitan areas throughout the country found that working families spend even more on transportation than on housing, a reflection of the "drive until you qualify" affordable housing strategy.[47] "In their search for low-cost housing, working families often locate far from their place of work, dramatically increasing their transportation costs and commute times." The unintended consequences do not stop there; this means less time with the family, increased traffic congestion for the region, and greater greenhouse gas emissions.

INFRASTRUCTURE AND ECONOMIC COMPETITIVENESS. Decentralized development has literally and figuratively sunk the infrastructure investment of the country into car-based transportation and other strung-out systems that are expensive to build and maintain and are often times used relatively lightly during the bulk of any given week. This massive infrastructure system may turn out to be too expensive to maintain.

The best-regarded work on the "costs of sprawl" is *Sprawl Costs,* by Robert Burchell of Rutgers University and Anthony Downs of The Brookings Institution. They summarized their research by saying, "The inefficiencies of sprawling development have become obvious for local governments trying to balance their budgets."[48] An example of these inefficiencies was brought to light by the massive regional planning effort in the Salt Lake City metropolitan area, called Envision Utah, that showed a savings of about twenty-five percent ($4.5 billion) in infrastructure costs over twenty years if somewhat more compact development occurred over that time period rather than the continuation of the current pattern of sprawling conventional development.[49, 50]

Most infrastructure categories, such as roads and sewer and water systems, have very high fixed costs. For example, the construction cost for building a mile of sewer line is reasonably similar in the suburbs and in the city. However, on a per-housing-unit basis, dividing that fixed cost over a small number of low-density houses means that it is far more expensive for each low-density house. If the taxes charged the homeowner to pay for the sewer line are similar for both low-density and high-density housing, as they tend to be, higher density walkable urbanism is massively subsidizing low-density drivable sub-urban development. For example, assume the sewer line costs $1 million per mile to build. If one mile of sewer line serves forty low-density houses in the suburbs, it costs $25,000 per house to install. If that mile of sewer line serves 400 high-density houses in a walkable urban place, it costs $2,500 per house.

The research comparing low-density drivable sub-urban development and higher density walkable urbanism clearly shows that "compact and contiguous development patterns are significantly more cost effective than those of a scattered and linear nature."[51] A 2004 Albuquerque assessment of the marginal cost of drivable sub-urban development found that it was twenty-two times more costly than walkable urban development for four infrastructure categories (roads, drainage, public safety, and parks).[52] Yet generally the taxes and fees mandated by municipal law dictate that all development, high density or low density, has to pay about the same. The result is that high-density development, as well as the general taxpayer, is subsidizing drivable sub-urbanism. It is just as if by law all restaurants have to be all-you-can-eat; those customers who eat very little subsidize those who eat a lot.

During a dinner conversation, a power company CEO was asked what it cost the company to build and service low-density development versus high-density development. He at first looked confused, then responded, "we don't look at our cost structure that way." Because his company is regulated by the state public utility commission, it adds up its costs and divides them evenly across the housing units that it serves, charging all residential users the same per kilowatt. There is no reason for the company to even worry about its marginal cost of doing business, something taught in accounting 101 during the first year of business school.

In the most recent "report card" on the fifteen categories of infrastructure in 2005, the American Society of Engineers (ASE) gave the country a "D," down from a "D+" from the last report card in 2001. The ASE's report, although certainly self-serving because the organization benefits from increased infrastructure investment, concluded, "Congested highways, overflowing sewers, and corroding bridges are constant reminders of the looming crisis that jeopardizes our nation's prosperity and our quality of life."[53] The society estimated that an additional $1.6 trillion is required over the next five years to minimally improve current conditions.

The very nature of drivable sub-urbanism's low-density infrastructure means that the country will always be in a catch-22 situation. Drivable sub-urbanism continually builds required new infrastructure, such as roads and sewer lines, to accommodate new growth, but we tend not to allocate enough funds to maintain what is already in place. It is a losing proposition that will eventually take a much larger toll on economic competitiveness. Even more troublesome is that the infrastructure is the wrong kind and in the wrong place for the demand generated by walkable urbanism, which needs *more* capacity in *fewer* locations. For example, we need larger and newer water lines in downtowns and suburban town centers, and significantly more investment in transit.

The dedication of a large portion of land in metropolitan areas to low-density housing and shopping malls means that land needed in the future for food production, wetland protection, and carbon sequestration will be difficult or impossible to assemble. If this extreme fringe of drivable sub-urban development becomes economically obsolete, due to soaring oil prices, market demand shift, or a change in national land-use policy, property values will drift downward, not justifying additional investment or maintenance. And because it is owned in many small parcels, this chopped up ownership pattern discourages any easy redevelopment, which is why land initially developed as drivable sub-urban tends to stay that way.

OIL DEPENDENCY AND POTENTIAL OF GLOBAL PEAK OIL. Drivable sub-urban development is based on cheap energy, specifically oil for the car-based transportation system. More than two-thirds of the oil used in the United States is used for transportation,[54] and there are presently no viable substitutes for oil in powering our cars, trucks, and planes, though many are being tried and researched. As Maryland Republican Roscoe Bartlett testified before his colleagues in the U.S. Congress, the United States has two percent of the world's oil reserves, produces eight percent of the world's oil annually (a figure that has been in decline absolutely and relatively for thirty-five years), has five percent of the world's population, and consumes twenty-five percent of the annual oil production. Congressman Bartlett said that this situation poses a historically "unprecedented risk management problem" for the country that could fundamentally disrupt our economy and way of life.[55]

As reported in a U.S. Department of Energy–funded report in 2005, there is a growing minority opinion that oil production is approaching or may even be at peak production worldwide,[56] just as the United States hit peak oil production in 1970. Chevron, the major oil company, had a massive advertising campaign in 2007 pointing this out to consumers. Whenever peak production is reached and the markets know for a fact that the supply will be on a future downward trajectory, the price will probably dramatically increase due to continued worldwide economic growth and demand for oil. For example, China recently passed Japan to become the second largest consumer of oil and is forecast to pass the United States in two decades. The future higher price for imported oil will put an even greater strain on the U.S. economy, compounding the continued balance of trade deficits, which are running at historically high levels (more than six percent of the gross domestic product) during the 2000s.[57]

The value of residential and commercial real estate that can be reached only by cars will certainly be significantly devalued when peak oil is reached, whenever that may be. The dollar will probably fall in value, making imported goods much more expensive, and the dollar may lose its status as the world's reserve currency. Some forecasters have suggested that peak oil, if it occurs without alternative energy sources under development, could trigger a global depression similar to the 1930s. The U.S. economy will have painted itself into a corner if peak oil arrives and the only option is drivable sub-urban development. James Kunstler, the author of *The Long Emergency*,[58] painted a bleak picture of the United States' future due to a "prodigious, unparalleled misallocation of resources" for drivable sub-urban development, which he forecasted will result in the collapse of the U.S. economy to a medieval level of output. Although Kunstler's is doubtless an extreme and overly pessimistic view, the trauma caused to the U.S. drivable sub-urban economy when peak oil is reached, particularly if this realization happens suddenly, which many forecasters predict is possible if not probable, would be severe. There is one conclusion on which nearly all oil production forecasters, including most of the major oil companies, agree: it is not a matter of whether peak oil production arrives, it is only a matter of when, and the majority of forecasters feel that the peak will occur in the first third of the twenty-first century.[59]

FOREIGN POLICY. As has been understood clearly only in the post–September 11th world, a significant unintended consequence of the drivable sub-urbanism domestic policy is its impact on foreign policy and the overarching need to maintain access to oil abroad. There are now more than 100 U.S. bases in the Middle East, almost all built within the past twenty years. Tom Friedman of the *New York Times* called it "petrolism—or petroleum-based politics."[60] Friedman recognized that the U.S. addiction to oil, primarily to maintain drivable sub-urbanism, fuels the very authoritarian regimes that support terrorism, against which U.S. foreign policy is fighting today. In Friedman's view, every gallon of gasoline purchased to maintain drivable sub-urbanism undermines U.S. foreign policy.

Michael O'Hanlon, a senior fellow at The Brookings Institution, estimated that at least twenty-five percent of the defense budget of $519 billion in fiscal year 2006 was spent in the Middle East, fighting the war in Iraq, protecting foreign governments' oil infrastructure, defending Israel, and patrolling oil shipping lanes.[61] Other estimates allocate upward of forty percent of the defense budget, or $200 billion, to the Middle East. If the $120 to $200 billion annually spent defending the Middle East were charged to domestic car and truck drivers in taxes, it would mean an additional $22 to $27 per barrel of oil or an additional $1.13 to $1.80 per gallon of gasoline.[62] This price increase would certainly bring a change in driving behavior and how we construct our built environment, not to mention significant political backlash. However, a Middle East defense tax on oil is not going to happen. What will happen is that the need for oil to fuel drivable sub-urbanism will continue to be a major factor in U.S. Middle East policy, a funding source for terrorism, and a growing influence on the United States' relationships with India and China as they seek to secure sources of oil.

In summary, the generally unintended but negative consequences of drivable sub-urbanism have come down to:

- automobile dependence, leaving us with essentially only one means of transportation
- social segregation
  concentration of poverty, which results in major social problems
  lack of access to jobs for many lower income and minority households
  exclusion of nondrivers from society—those too old, too young, too poor, disabled, or not interested
  secession of the elites, propelling the growth of a two-class society
  NIMBY neighborhood groups, trained to oppose drivable sub-urban development
- environmental effects
  land consumption at probably ten to twenty times the underlying population growth
  heat islands due to so much land under asphalt
  water quality degradation due to the runoff from all that asphalt

air quality degradation in spite of emission controls due to geometric growth in automobile use

climate change due to the unproven but intuitive connection between low-density, car-based development and greenhouse gas emissions

- health implications

respiratory diseases

asthma

obesity

increased car accidents

- economic effects

strained personal finances as American households have shifted more of their spending to maintaining their fleet of depreciable cars

declining infrastructure and economic competitiveness, due to building relatively lightly used, spread-out infrastructure that is too expensive to maintain and is massively subsidized, affecting all sorts of choices

oil dependency and the potential of global peak oil, which has significant impact on the huge trade deficit today and potentially serious implications when the peak in oil production is reached

foreign policy implications, because our oil purchases subsidize our enemies.

TRADE-OFFS BETWEEN THE POSITIVE AND NEGATIVE CONSEQUENCES OF DRIVABLE SUB-URBANISM

With any social engineering experiment, the initial focus tends to be on the personal and societal benefits, causing great excitement and raising expectations. There is no reason to even consider proceeding with such an experiment if there are no anticipated benefits. Given the nearly spiritual longing stirred by Futurama, American society considered only the upsides of the experiment, which is not unusual at all. Very few voices hinted at what might be lost by fundamentally throwing overboard 5,500 years of experience in constructing the built environment.

Yet, as explained in this chapter, the price has been great. However, even if we somehow foresaw these unintended consequences, we probably would have still chosen Futurama and drivable sub-urbanism in the middle of the twentieth century. The emotional allure of Futurama lined up with the economic benefits of an automobile-driven economy, so it was easy to believe in the dream. But now, perhaps, the United States is waking up to a new economic and environmental reality.

5

THE MARKET REDISCOVERS
WALKABLE URBANISM

For better and for worse, the now middle-aged baby boomers were the first generation to grow up on television. This huge age cohort was raised on *Leave It to Beaver* in the late 1950s, the *Dick Van Dyke Show* in the early 1960s, and *The Brady Bunch* in the early 1970s, some of the most popular situation comedies of the era. These shows had one thing in common; they were all set in the suburbs. The unifying subtext of these series was the appeal and desirability of suburban living. All of the main characters, from the Cleaver family to Mike and Carol Brady, lived in single-family houses in picture-perfect drivable sub-urbanism. The optimism of the era came through with every episode as dogs were lost and found, teenage romances bloomed and faded, and work issues that were brought home got resolved hilariously. The warm glow of a happy ending descended at the end of each thirty-minute show. This was how life was meant to be.

The setting of nearly all situation comedies of the era in the suburbs was not an accident. The media entertainment industry (movies, television, music, and now video games) conducts more consumer research than probably any other industry. Television shows in particular are barometers of how Americans want to see themselves, even if it does not reflect their current life. In the '50s, '60s and '70s, Americans obviously wanted to see themselves as living a drivable sub-urban life, relishing the joys and not concerning themselves with the then-unrecognized unintended consequences. After the travails and ultimate success of fighting World War II, suburban life was the best of all possible worlds—the epitome of the American Dream for that age.

Fast forward to the 1990s and early 2000s to see the most popular television shows of that era—*Seinfeld, Friends,* and *Sex in the City*—all set in the city. The unifying subtext of these series was the appeal and desirability of walkable urbanism. Even though only forty-one percent of all residents in metropolitan areas in 1990 lived in their central city, one of the main, although not the only location of walkable urbanism, television research and viewership indicated a desire to at least watch their favorite characters live and work in walkable urban places. Gatherings of young adults in restaurants and apartments on these shows made urban life exciting and engaging and offered that most attractive attribute of that era—being hip.

These shows were also significant for what they did not portray: urban violence. A single woman would saunter down the street at night on the way to an art gallery opening in a former industrial section, as imagined by the television writer and portrayed on the screen, without a sense of foreboding. It was safe, exciting, hip, and the place to be if you were young and on the way up.

Even as edgeless cities were pushing growth ever outward, the popular appeal of urban life was growing. Although subtle at first, the 1990s witnessed a revival in many American downtowns, spurred in part, no doubt, by the dramatic drop in urban crime in the 1990s. There were also signs of new walkable urban places being developed in some suburban town centers, new development around transit stations, and new walkable development built from scratch on greenfields, places where walkable urban development takes place on land previously used as farm land. At first this development started slowly in the mid- and late 1990s, but it took off in the 2000s. The New Urbanism movement sparked much of this generally suburban-located development.

So the middle of the 2000s decade found the country going in two, diametrically opposed directions. The majority of housing and commercial development was still heading for the hills, pushing the fringe like it has never been pushed before. Metropolitan areas were expanding geometrically as farms were converted into subdivisions named after what they replaced—Whispering Woods, Bubbling Brook, Woodmont. Yet a countertrend had certainly started with downtowns reviving and transit- and nontransit-served suburban town centers taking off with new development, revitalization, and excitement.

Many contemporary observers of the built environment, such as Joel Kotkin, Robert Bruegmann, and David Brooks, feel the rediscovery of walkable urbanisn is at best a small niche, at worst a Yuppie fad that will soon fade. Kotkin disdainfully referred to downtown revitalization as a "Potemkin strategy" producing a "boutique city" for the "so-called creative class." These critics generally feel that drivable sub-urban development is the continuation of thousands of years of sprawl. Mankind has always wanted more space, they say, and had a desire to be away from other humans, and the car was just the next step in that millennia-old progression.

So what is it going to be over the next generation: continued low-density, drivable sub-urbanism or a shift to compact walkable urbanism or some combination of the two?

I argue that demographic trends, consumer preferences, an emerging new version of the American Dream, and recognition of the consequences of drivable sub-urbanism are all pushing the pendulum back. The United States is on the verge of a new phase in constructing its built environment.

A NEW AMERICAN DREAM EMERGES

There are a few major factors at work in how we construct the built environment, according to Arthur C. Nelson in a wide-ranging study in the *Journal of the American Planning Association* in late 2006.[1] First, as has been the case since the middle of the twentieth century, is the aging of the baby boomers. Much has been written about the boomers in each stage of their aging. Current trends show that empty nesters and retirees tend to downsize their housing. University of Southern California researchers found that people more than fifty-five years old are three times more likely than people in their midtwenties and early thirties to choose a townhouse in the city as the best living option.[2]

The impact of the retiring baby boomers has yet to be felt in the 2000s. Only in the early- to mid-2010s will their crossing the age sixty-five boundary begin to affect society. About 350,000 Americans turned sixty-five each year from 2000 to 2006. From 2007 to 2011, more than twice that number will turn sixty-five—about 800,000 people each year. Between 2012 and 2020, an average of 1,500,000 will turn sixty-five each year-more than four times the number in the early 2000s. As always, the tidal wave of the baby boomers will change America's institutions, and the probable impact on the built environment will be a demand for more walkable urban housing.

The type of family for whom the typical drivable sub-urban home was built—two parents, stay-at-home mom, 2.5 kids—is no longer the American norm. Aging baby boomers were mostly empty nesters in the mid-2000s; younger people are starting their families later, and families tend to be smaller. As a result there is a decline in the number of households with children living in the home. In 1960, nearly half of all households included children living in the home. This fell to thirty-three percent in 2000, and it is expected to continue to decline to twenty-eight percent in 2025. Households with school-age children, which are a major determinant of housing choice, stand at an even lower percentage. This means that growth in households will be driven by empty nesters, never-nesters, and singles. The last category has been and will continue to be the biggest recent societal change; single households will equal the number of families with children by 2025, each making up twenty-eight percent of all households.

However, change happens on the margin. As Nelson pointed out, the absolute growth of households will be from 108 million households in

2000 to 140 million in 2025. The number of households *with* children is projected to grow only 4 million (from 35 million to 39 million households), a mere twelve percent of the total absolute increase. The number of households *without* children is projected to grow by 28 million (73 million to 101 million households), eighty-eight percent of the total increase. Those additional 28 million childless households, more than seven times the absolute growth of families with children, will be the primary factor that dictates the future of the built environment. These households will not overly concern themselves with the quality of public schools or the perceived need for large lots for children in making their decisions. This fact will open up many possibilities. More couples and singles will be motivated to continue the revival of many downtowns and downtown-adjacent parts of major American cities, as they have in the late 1990s and early 2000s, and they will look to development in greenfield suburban town centers built from scratch as well as to traditional walkable urbanism, and everything in between. Another study, "The Coming Demand," predicted that basic demographic changes will lead dense, walkable neighborhoods to gain market share over the coming decades, although changing preferences could significantly expand that market.[3]

The age of *Leave It to Beaver* is over, replaced by the era of *Seinfeld*.

Another factor is at work in Americans' shifting demand from drivable sub-urbanism to walkable urbanism: boredom. Remember the "choices" referred to in chapter 1? A single-family home or a single-family home? A 1980s or 1990s strip mall in which to shop for groceries? With so few choices, boredom is bound to set in. This was the case in the 1950s when only run-down walkable urbanism was available; the market was bored with only one choice. The late sociologist Robert Nisbet was convinced that boredom is a major cause in motivating societal actions—people got bored with the negative consequences. The boredom of having only the option of drivable sub-urban life, including the unintended consequences of ever longer and more congested commutes and the running of nearly every errand in a car, is not to be underestimated.

Alongside these demographic changes, the economy has made a fundamental change. The new economy has been called many things: the virtual economy, the service economy, the postindustrial economy, the knowledge economy, and the creative economy. This has come to mean a focus on the up front, creative portion of a product or service development and the back-end marketing and distribution of that product or service. The actual production may be outsourced abroad, or it may be accomplished with fewer employees in this country due to advances in technology, which lead to increased productivity. This is a repeat of the earlier trend of increased productivity in agriculture, leading to plummeting numbers of jobs over the past century (agricultural jobs were down to less than two percent of all jobs in 2000 from, as mentioned in chapter 1, forty percent in 1900 and twenty-seven percent in 1920). The agricultural economy transitioned to the industrial economy, and now the industrial is transitioning to the knowledge economy. The economic driver of how the American Dream is implemented on the ground is changing once again.

Dr. Richard Florida's assertion in his 2002 book, *The Rise of the Creative Class,* that future economic growth depends on the retention and attraction of the highly educated has become accepted wisdom of many economic development officials in cities throughout the country. The breeding and attraction of young, highly educated people to start new companies, attract similar entrepreneurs, build the local tax base, and become more "hip" is driving many urban and suburban economic development strategies in the 2000s. *The Economist* magazine reported that "talent has become the world's most sought after commodity."[4] Certainly not all of the so-called creative class—software engineers; medical, legal, and financial professionals; high-tech entrepreneurs; educators; and others—want to live in walkable urban places for all phases of their lives, but many of them certainly want the opportunity to do so and may demand it at various times of their lives. The metropolitan area that does not offer walkable urbanism is probably destined to lose economic development opportunities; the creative class will gravitate to those metro areas that offer multiple choices in living arrangements.

The growth of the knowledge economy means that the most important factor in determining which metropolitan areas experience growth in new companies and jobs is the quality of the workforce—their education, training, and experience. The metropolitan areas with the highest educational attainment tend to be the fastest growing regions today—witness the growth of the two coasts and the Sunbelt of the past couple of decades, the new "U" shape of the USA. This highly educated workforce has lots of choices in how and where they live. Having communities built only according to the Futurama-inspired American Dream is no longer enough. Yes, many families in certain phases of their life want drivable sub-urbanism. But there is pent-up demand for walkable urbanism, spanning from the low key 1950s Hill Valley on one end of the spectrum to the intense buzz of Midtown Manhattan on the other, and many versions in between. However, there is insufficient supply. The issues revolve around providing choice and ample supply of walkable urbanism. A one-size-fits-all version of the current Futurama-inspired American Dream is no longer enough.

RECENT CONSUMER PREFERENCE RESEARCH

The shifting demographics are only one part of the story. What Americans say they want is shifting as well. Studies using a technique that analyzes the trade-offs people make in choosing where to live show that a significant segment of the population wants something different from the standard, conforming drivable products that the real estate industry is geared to provide them. In particular, these studies focused on not just the house in isolation, but the entire community and the way life would be lived there.

Anton Nelessen, a Princeton-based researcher and professor at Rutgers University, began these trade-off studies in the 1980s and 1990s. He invented a methodology he called "visual preference surveys." He asked consumers to rate a series of two contrasting photographs from the general geographic area where they lived; the first photos showed drivable suburban places (e.g., a strip mall, a large-lot single-family house, a business park) and the second photos showed the same uses but in a walkable urban condition (e.g., a Main Street shopping area; higher density single-family housing on a smaller lot; a vibrant, walkable business district). The vast majority of people taking Nelessen's survey preferred walkable places over drivable sub-urban places. It must have been one of the most boring surveys to administer because Nelessen found the same results time and time again. As he wrote after conducting 50,000 individual surveys across the country, "In general, I have found that most people reject the current pattern and spatial characteristics of sprawl in favor of more traditional or neo-traditional small [walkable urban] communities."[5] These surveys were not scientific, as the participants were self-selected. They are also not necessarily an endorsement of the range of walkable urban places that could exist, particularly because few new walkable places existed in the 1980s and early 1990s when these surveys were conducted. Yet they showed an overwhelming preference—eighty-eight percent of those sur-veyed—for something other than drivable sub-urbanism and for places that were more walkable and had many uses in close proximity.

Studies and surveys completed in the 2000s have found more com-pelling evidence that a market exists for walkable urbanism. Dr. Jona-than Levine of the University of Michigan and colleagues[6] conducted research in two very different metropolitan areas, Boston and Atlanta, to understand consumer preference for walkable urbanism and drivable sub-urbanism. He surveyed more than 1,600 people, scientifically rep-resentative of the metropolitan areas as a whole, asking participants to choose between two scenarios to clarify the types of trade-offs consum-ers make. Questions included:

I like living in a neighborhood with single-family houses on larger lots, even if this means that public transportation is not available.

Versus

I like living in a neighborhood with a good bus and train system, even if it means a neighborhood with a mix of single-family houses and multi-family buildings that are close together.

FIGURE 5.1. Survey respondents in the Levine research saw a picture of this sidewalk café in Atlanta as an example of walkable urban retail development. (Source: Aseem Inam)

Another example of the trade-off questions Dr. Levine used is:

I like living in a neighborhood where people (figure 5.1) can walk to places like stores, libraries, or restaurants, even if this means that the houses and stores are within a block or two of one another.

Versus

I like living in a neighborhood (figure 5.2) where the commercial areas are kept far from houses, even if this means that people can't walk to places like stores, libraries or restaurants.

The results showed a demand for walkable urbanism by twenty-nine percent of respondents in Atlanta and forty percent in Boston, versus a demand for drivable sub-urbanism of forty-one percent in Atlanta and thirty percent in Boston. The remaining approximately thirty percent of the residents in both metro areas fell somewhere in between and could have accepted either option or did not know what they wanted. These two

FIGURE 5.2. Survey respondents in the Levine research saw a picture of this sub-urban Atlanta home as an example of drivable sub-urban residential development. (Source: Aseem Inam)

metro areas could conceivably reflect the extremes of the country as a whole regarding housing and lifestyle options; Atlanta is primarily a postwar, car-dominated region, while Boston is an older metropolitan area with a significant rail transit system that has been in place for more than a century. This could mean that in the country as a whole roughly thirty to forty percent of people want walkable urbanism, thirty to forty percent want drivable sub-urbanism, and thirty percent are willing to accept either. Dividing the "agnostics" arbitrarily in half leaves forty-five to fifty-five percent of the market wanting or willing to accept walkable urbanism and the other forty-five to fifty-five percent wanting or willing to accept drivable sub-urbanism. Like so much in American life and politics over the past generation, there may be a split down the middle in how we want to live.

The amount of walkable urban housing *supply* in the Boston and Atlanta metropolitan areas shows a tremendous disparity. The Levine research showed that seventy percent of the Boston respondents who wanted walkable urbanism actually got this kind of housing, while only thirty-five percent of the respondents in Atlanta who wanted to live in a walkable urban place were able to find and afford it. In contrast, the vast majority of the people who wanted drivable sub-urbanism got that choice in both regions—ninety-five percent in Atlanta and eighty-five percent in Boston. Based upon the Levine research, there is significant pent-up demand for more walkable urban product, particularly in places like Atlanta.

Jonathan Levine and his colleague Lawrence Frank undertook a further in-depth examination of the Atlanta consumer research data to determine if those who were presently living in drivable sub-urban places had a preference for walkable urbanism. Levine and Frank found "evidence that the segment of the housing market that is interested in [compact, mixed-use, accessible development oriented toward walking, cycling, or transit] is under-served . . . there is unmet demand."[7] In the Levine and Frank study, between twenty and forty percent of those surveyed who lived in a drivable sub-urban home had a very strong preference for compact and walkable neighborhoods that allow short commutes and transportation options. Yet at the time of the survey in 2002, only about one in twenty homes in the Atlanta area met that criteria. About one-third of residents living in drivable sub-urbia would prefer walkable communities, but could not find such neighborhoods with good schools and low crime.[8]

Another consumer survey, conducted for the National Association of Realtors and Smart Growth America, found that many people are actively looking for alternatives. The survey found that fifty-five percent of prospective homebuyers want a home with a mix of single-family and other higher density housing, sidewalks, shops, schools, and public transit within walking distance. The other forty-five percent wanted single-family homes on large lots, with all services drivable, and no transit.[9]

RCLCo, a national real estate advisory firm, concluded in a presentation to national homebuilders and the U.S. Environmental Protection Agency in 2007, based upon their national consumer research studies, that "one third of the consumer real estate market prefers smart growth development" (another term for walkable urbanism and defined by RCLCo as "new urbanism, transit oriented development and urban and suburban in-fill") and that "there is no doubt the size of the market is growing." The RCLCo conclusions were gathered from twelve in-depth, scientific consumer research surveys of thousands of individuals in metropolitan areas such as Atlanta, Phoenix, Charlotte, Chattanooga, Orlando, Albuquerque, and Boise—hardly old-line eastern cities with transit systems.

WHAT PEOPLE ARE ACTUALLY DOING

The consumer research discussed above shows what respondents *say* they want. However, there is ample evidence of what households actually *do* on the pages of most Sunday newspaper real estate sections throughout the country. The best comparative evidence of the pent-up demand for walkable urbanism is the price per square foot consumers are actually paying for higher density housing in walkable urban places versus drivable suburban single-family housing in similar parts of the same metropolitan area. These data provide hard evidence that the market is willing to pay a significant premium for walkable urbanism; this is not just theoretical demographic and consumer research.

In Birmingham, Michigan, a walkable urban-suburban town in the economically depressed Detroit metropolitan area, the average selling price per square foot for a downtown condo (priced between $750,000 and $1,500,000) was $445 per square foot in 2007.[10] A drivable sub-urban house a few minutes away by car but still in Birmingham in the same absolute price range cost $318 per square foot. In the Detroit region, one of the least walkable metro areas in the country, primarily due to its extreme dependence on car manufacturing, there is a forty percent price premium for walkable urbanism ($127 per foot walkable urban premium over the drivable sub-urban base price).

In the Denver metropolitan area in 2007, luxury homes priced between $750,000 and $1,500,000 in Highland Ranch, a single-family master-planned community, sell for an average price of about $195 per square foot. However, if one wanted to enjoy the walkable urbanism that over the past decade has exploded in downtown Denver, a comparably priced luxury home will cost about $487 per foot, a 150 percent premium (one and a half times the price per square foot). High-end households seem to be willing to pay the same absolute dollars for a 4,000–7,000-square-foot suburban palace near golf courses and behind guard gates as they pay for condominiums in downtown that are about a third the size but have a city view and walking access to the best selection of restaurants in the region and maybe even to work.

This premium for walkable urban housing is also seen in the Seattle area suburban town of Kirkland, hardly a historic hotbed of walkable urbanism. Kirkland drivable sub-urban housing costs $358 per square foot, while walkable urban condominiums are priced at $540 per square foot. This is a fifty-one percent premium.

The New York City metropolitan area probably has the most extreme premiums for walkable urban housing in the country. In wealthy Westchester County, north of New York City, a drivable, single-family home, priced between $1 and $2 million in 2007, translates into $365 per square foot. If you want the walkable pleasures of downtown White Plains, the major suburban city in the county, you would pay a 100 percent premium (twice the price per square foot or $750) for a condominium over a single-family house. However, if you want the excitement of Manhattan, it will cost you on average $1,064 per square foot, a 200 percent premium (a three-fold premium) over a drivable single-family house in Westchester County. It is possible that the extreme premiums paid in New York City for walkable urban housing may be where the country as a whole is going, not on an absolute price per square foot basis but from a relative premium perspective.[11]

Another sign of the actual shift toward walkable urbanism is that condominium prices have been rising substantially more than the prices for single-family houses in the early and mid-2000s. Condos have for previous generations been the low-cost means of getting into the housing market. As a result, not all condos were built in walkable urban places;

many built in the 1980s and 1990s are still the affordable alternative to a single-family detached house and are on the fringe of the metropolitan area, which means that the owners have to drive everywhere. However, enough high-priced walkable urban condos have been built, redeveloped, or just appreciated in value over the past fifteen years that this has forced the national average condo price up dramatically. The trend accelerated in the early- to mid-2000s; condos appreciated at almost twice the rate of single-family housing between 2002 and 2005. In 2003 average sales prices per square foot for condominiums were more than detached housing units for the first time in the country's history.[12] It was not long ago that a condominium was the entry-level product you bought if you could not afford a "real" house, meaning single-family detached.

These examples indicate that housing prices in walkable urban places have about a 40–200 percent (three-fold) premium over drivable single-family housing, controlling for price range and luxury orientation of the housing. Although there is no national study of walkable urban sales prices versus prices in comparable drivable sub-urban places, it is likely that vibrant walkable urban places will have the highest housing prices in the competitive market area. If that vibrant walkable urban place is in or adjacent to the traditional downtown, prices there will probably be the highest in the entire metropolitan area. These statements could not have been made ten to twenty years ago, reflecting the dramatic shift in values that has taken place over that period of time as walkable urban development began to reassert itself. In a New York Times story about small efficiency condominiums across the country in early 2007, the wife of a couple who had recently purchased a tiny 320-square-foot unit in downtown Charleston, South Carolina, remarked that she always wanted to live downtown, "but of course the closer I got to the city center, the higher the cost."[13] That would have been an unbelievable statement in 1990; downtown housing was for the poor and others who had few options. Because the pent-up demand for walkable urbanism will probably not be fully met over the next ten to twenty years, these price premiums will probably just increase. This is the reason that the extreme relative situation in the New

York metropolitan area, where there is a 200 percent premium for walkable urban product over drivable sub-urban, may be a precursor for the rest of the country in the near future.

It is important to mention, given the decline in the housing market in general throughout the nation as I am writing this book, that most housing prices have been static or falling throughout much of the country in 2006 and 2007. The question, which will be understood only in retrospect, is which type of housing will fall least and which type will see prices and sales pace increase first and fastest when the housing market picks up—walkable urban or drivable sub-urban? A private RCLCo analysis compared the 2006 (a year of housing weakness) for-sale housing market in the Washington, D.C., metro area to 2005 (the peak year of recent housing strength). It showed relatively flat prices and a slight decline (twelve percent) in sales pace for the District of Columbia and Arlington County, Virginia, both places with an abundance of walkable urban housing. In the far fringe of the D.C. metropolitan area (Loudon, Fauquier, and Prince William counties in Virginia), where nearly all housing is drivable sub-urban, sales prices were also relatively flat, but the sales pace had declined approximately thirty-five percent.[14] The fringe drivable sub-urban housing appears to be most severely affected by the market downturn in the Washington region, but only time will tell for certain.

A Bloomberg news story in early 2007 reported that Toll Brothers, the largely suburban luxury single-family home builder, felt that the housing market was "pretty much a bust" and the company could not predict when the recovery would begin. However, Toll Brothers had started a walkable urban housing division in 2006, and Bloomberg reported that "a bright spot has been the company's urban developments in cities, including Hoboken, New Jersey" (across the Hudson River from Manhattan). Robert Toll, the chief executive officer of the company, said, "We're killing them in Hoboken. . . ."[15] meaning sales were great.

Few seem to realize that the relatively higher housing sales prices for walkable urban real estate, as compared to drivable sub-urban, are a sign of market preference. The disparity in prices signals that there is more demand for walkable urbanism than the real estate industry can produce. Because walkable urbanism is mainly illegal by zoning, is difficult to finance, and the industry does not yet fully understand how to develop it, the supply has been insufficient. There are no definitive studies of how much supply of walkable urban product exists. However, I believe that metropolitan areas such as Atlanta and Phoenix have no more than ten percent of their housing supply in walkable urban neighborhoods. Older metropolitan areas such as Boston and Chicago may have upward of twenty to thirty percent of their housing in walkable urban neighborhoods. This lack of supply of walkable urban product, compared to the demand by at least thirty to forty percent of households reported above, drives up the price of the existing walkable stock. Yet, households apparently are willing to pay the substantial premium demanded for it.

PENT-UP DEMAND FOR COMMERCIAL WALKABLE URBANISM

The preference for walkable urbanism is not confined to housing. In an analysis of the Washington, D.C., regional office market conducted by RCLCo, walkable urban office space in late 2006 leased for twenty-seven percent more than drivable sub-urban space ($37.56 per square foot annual rent for walkable urban versus $29.67 for drivable sub-urban, or a premium of $7.89 per square foot). In addition, walkable urban space also had a much lower vacancy rate (7.7 percent), than drivable space (11.5 percent). The prime walkable urban office location is in downtown D.C., where office rents average $50 per square foot (some space is more than $60 per square foot), which makes this area the second highest office rental market in the country after Midtown Manhattan.[16] The prime drivable sub-urban office location is Tysons Corner in Virginia, where office rents average $31 per square foot. Office space in walkable downtown rents for a sixty-one percent premium ($19 per square foot downtown premium) over drivable sub-urban Tysons Corner.[17] In other words, office decision makers are willing to pay more to have their workers and themselves be able to walk to lunch, meet people on the street, and, probably most importantly, provide the options of taking transit or walking to work, as well as driving.

In Reston Town Center, one of the few nontransit-served walkable urban places in the Washington, D.C., region, rental rates for office, retail, and apartment space are all about fifty percent higher than comparable space that is only drivable in Reston, according to an internal Brookings Institution study.[18] Condominium sales prices are also about fifty percent higher. Obviously companies and households are willing to pay a significant premium to be able to walk to lunch, from home to work, from work to the store, and just to stroll along the urban avenues. Some drivable office, retail, and apartment competition may be only a half mile away, but that requires getting into a car, and the market expects to get a discount if you cannot walk to the urban amenities of Reston Town Center.

LAND IS WHERE PENT-UP DEMAND RESIDES

The inflated price for walkable urbanism is really a reflection of the higher price of the land under the condos, townhouses, small-lot single-family houses, offices, and apartments in these communities. High-density construction does cost more per square foot, but that does not entirely explain why walkable urban housing prices per square foot are 40–200 percent greater than for homes in drivable sub-urban areas, as shown in the above examples. The main reason for these large price differentials is in the land,[19] which is where the true supply/demand imbalance settles.

Land values in walkable urban places as a percentage of the total house price are much higher than in drivable sub-urban places. The lot under a single-family house in the Detroit suburbs will be around twenty percent of the house value. In contrast, the land under the condo in downtown walkable urban Birmingham, Michigan, will be about thirty-three percent of the condo value. In the Washington, D.C., suburbs, the land under a single-family house that one can only drive to on the fringe of the region is about thirty percent of the house price, while the land under a townhouse in walkable urban Dupont Circle is about fifty percent of the total value. In a balanced market, where there is no pent-up demand for any one kind of development, land under a condo in a walkable urban place should be about the same as that under a drivable sub-urban house.

That land value is a much greater percentage for walkable urban real estate shows that the supply/demand imbalance is pretty extreme. It is also a reflection of how walkability acts as a natural "governor" on the real estate market. If a walkable distance is defined as 1,500–3,000 feet—an area roughly 200–500 acres in size—that limits how much can be built. In drivable sub-urban development, there is effectively no governor on how much product can be added. Walkable urbanism means that there is an edge to the walkable district by controlling overbuilding.

This land value imbalance also shows where the profit will be made in real estate as developers strive to convert low-density suburban places into walkable urban places. When there is excess demand for one type of development, such as exists with walkable urbanism, the price of land spikes upward, causing windfall profits for some and unaffordable housing for many. Correcting this imbalance will be *the* major market force affecting the real estate industry for the next few decades as the pent-up demand is gradually satisfied, as will be further addressed in chapter 7.

The Washington, D.C., metropolitan area is an early example of the sea change taking place as the market shifts from drivable sub-urban development to walkable urbanism, as many drivable sub-urban places are converting to walkable urban places. For example, there has been a steady increase over the past twenty years in the percentage of residential building permits going to attached housing (townhomes and condominiums), which is what makes up most walkable urban housing. In the 1980s, fifteen percent of all building permits were for attached housing; this increased to twenty-two percent in the 1990s and to twenty-six percent in the 2000s.[20] There were two walkable urban places in the D.C. region in the 1980s (Georgetown and Old Town Alexandria, both eighteenth-century colonial towns with strong tourist support). In 2007, there are seventeen walkable places, with at least five more emerging, as will be discussed in more depth in the next chapter.

HOW LONG WILL IT TAKE TO SATISFY THE PENT-UP DEMAND FOR WALKABLE URBANISM?

The built environment takes far longer to turn than the proverbial supertanker. According to the U.S. Census Bureau, the country has been adding about $1.2 trillion dollars in new construction (this does not count rehabilitations, so it undercounts total construction spending) to the built environment each year during the mid-2000s.[21] As mentioned in the Introduction, thirty-five percent of the assets of the U.S. economy is invested in the built environment (real estate and infrastructure), which translates into about $70 trillion. We are conservatively adding 1.7 percent to the asset base per year, so rounding up to 2.0 percent is reasonable.[22]

Arthur C. Nelson wrote in his paper, "The Longer View," published in the *Journal of the American Planning Association,* that, "More than $30 trillion will be spent on development between the period 2000 and 2025. Nearly 50 million new homes will be built, including some 16 million that will be rebuilt or replaced entirely with other land uses. Seventy-five billion square feet of nonresidential space will be built with 60 billion [square feet] replacing space that existed in 2000: New nonresidential development will equal all such development that existed in 2000."[23]

This is a tremendous amount of development that, if it follows current asset allocation, will require around thirty-five percent of American investment capital during that period. This would be the largest portion the country will invest in any asset class—more than government and corporate research and development, more than all of the capital investment in publicly traded companies, and more than the country's defense spending. Yet this change will take longer to implement than, for example, completely replacing the fleet of cars and trucks on the roads today. Long-term planning is essential if the United States and its huge and crucial investment in the built environment are to be properly positioned for the economic and environmental challenges of the twenty-first century.

Given the zoning laws, the financing that is in place today, and the skill of the development industry, it would stand to reason that the vast majority of this huge growth would be built as a continuation of drivable sub-urbanism. Arthur C. Nelson asserted in his paper that this would be a mistake. Employing the recent trade-off analysis consumer research, such as the Levine and Frank research, and demographic changes mentioned above, he concluded that nearly all of the housing and much of the commercial product should be high-density product suitable for walkable urbanism—or face early obsolescence.

Nelson's "probable" case scenario showed that between 2000 and 2030, there will be a thirty-two percent increase in the number of rental apartment units (8 million new units added to the 25 million existing units in 2000), a 175 percent increase in attached for-sale units (21 million new units added to the 12 million existing units in 2000), and a sixty-two percent increase in small-lot detached houses (25 million new units versus the 40 million existing units in 2000). All of these new units have the potential to be built in walkable urban places, though probably not all of them will be.

The shocking conclusion of the Nelson research in his probable case scenario was that about forty-one percent of all large-lot single-family houses existing in 2000, presumably most if not all of them in drivable sub-urban locations, will go begging for buyers. There were 54 million large-lot single-family houses in 2000 and Nelson projects that upward of 22 million will not find ready buyers when it comes time to sell, which implies much lower prices. The premiums for walkable urban housing cited above (40–200 percent) may be achieved at the expense of large-lot single-family homes, because this type of house will probably decline in value. Nelson's numbers show that it will take until 2030 and probably even longer to get the inherently slow-to-change real estate market to correct the current shortage of high-density, walkable urban real estate product.

CAN THE REAL ESTATE INDUSTRY AND WALL STREET ADAPT?

The real estate development industry, particularly the part of the industry financed by conventional sources such as Wall Street and national commercial banks, has not been fully aware of these current and future changes. Much of the new product that satisfies the demand for walkable urbanism has been built by small and midsized companies—for example, devotees of New Urbanism and firms deeply committed to downtown revitalization and historic rehabilitation, which I guess to be no more than twenty percent of the industry. Yet awareness is dawning. A 2004 survey conducted of the members of the Urban Land Institute, the most prestigious and respected international real estate research and trade association, found that they believe there is a market for these alternatives, but that municipal regulations remain the primary barrier to meeting this growing demand.

Perhaps most encouragingly, some change is taking place in the standard product types that define most real estate activity. A couple of possible walkable urban standard real estate products introduced during the 2000s are being accepted by Wall Street. Before 2000, these product types were not standard and were being produced only by pioneering developers who generally had a very hard time obtaining financing. Wall Street and other financers can certainly change; it just takes them some time to collect data on how the new product types have performed in the market.

The pent-up demand for walkable urbanism first made itself obvious to rental apartment developers. Younger Generation X and Y households are more attracted to walkable living than probably any segment of the population, and these households are more likely to rent (these are the folks who watched *Seinfeld* and *Friends*). Therefore, the demand for walkable urban rental apartments began to take off in the 1990s as downtowns and other walkable urban places revived. These projects generally use three-and four-story wood-frame construction with elevators and reinforced concrete structured parking. Many times the structured parking is "buried" behind the apartment units, hidden from the street. Construction

FIGURE 5.3. What has come to be called "Texas apartments" surround parking that is "buried" in the middle of the block. These high-density apartments were pioneered in Uptown Dallas by Robert Shaw, the chief executive officer of a small development firm eventually acquired by Post Properties, Inc., a New York Stock Exchange real estate investment trust. Uptown is a walkable urban place, immediately adjacent to downtown Dallas, that pioneered the revival of walkable urbanism in the Dallas metropolitan area. (Source: Post Properties, Inc., Steve Hinds Photography, 2007)

of this kind of unit costs more than standard garden apartments, and the reinforced concrete parking garages costs much more than surface parking or individual wood-frame garages employed in garden apartments. In metropolitan areas with higher costs, there is also a market shift to higher density reinforced concrete apartments (figure 5.3) that are more than four stories high, supported by reinforced concrete parking decks. This is the most expensive construction used today for rental housing and must receive a significant rental price premium to justify their construction. So this kind of construction and density can be justified only in New York, Boston, Washington, Chicago, Los Angeles, Seattle, and similar cities. These two forms of urban density apartments are now part of the nineteen standard product types.

FIGURE 5.4. Lifestyle centers is a new retail concept of an open-air "Main Street" with stores facing the sidewalks. Initial lifestyle centers were retail only, as shown here, but have become more mixed-use in the late 2000s with housing and office on the floors above the retail. (Source: David Ruffo)

Another new standard product is the strange-sounding retail category of "Lifestyle Center." It is a pseudo-Main Street; a two-lane street with "teaser" parking on one or both sides of the street, regional and national retail stores built up to the sidewalks, and a sea of surface parking surrounding the place where most of the customers park. It is Disney-like in nature—a suburban theme park—but it begins to provide a sense of community in an otherwise sterile suburban place. One of the first in the country was The Avenue at Whitemarsh, in suburban Baltimore, located across a four-lane arterial from the Whitemarsh Mall, the largest regional mall in Maryland. The Avenue is surrounded by asphalt parking lots with the Main Street retail stores facing one another, anchored by a twenty-screen movie theater, a national book store, regional and national chain restaurants, kitchen and accessory stores, and coffee shops. There are outdoor sidewalk cafes and a fountain in the center, and the place is heavily hyped and programmed to feel like it is the "downtown" of its drivable sub-urban area. The lifestyle center is the new home to Santa at Christmas. It is where children's birthday parties are held. There are parades down Main Street on major holidays. In essence, lifestyle centers have taken the place of new regional malls on the list of nineteen standard real estate products. Very few regional malls are now being built, but they are not going away and some of them may be expanded. However, many regional and national retail chains now prefer to locate in open-air lifestyle centers (figure 5.4). As a result, though, as one could easily guess, lifestyle centers are beginning to look very much alike. Commodification strikes again.

Both urban high-density apartments and lifestyle centers still are single use, so they don't meet the basic test of walkable urbanism—the ability to walk out the door and find many things to do within walking distance. However, that may be changing. According to an internal Brookings Institution study, before 2006, eighty percent of the lifestyle centers were retail only, like The Avenue at Whitemarsh.[24] However, about two-thirds of the projects that are being planned for delivery in the late 2000s have housing and/or office space over the retail, a major change for the development and finance community. One of the best examples of this new trend is West Village (figure 5.5), which is in the walkable urban Uptown section adjacent to downtown Dallas. It has upscale retail with luxury rental apartments built above. No one developer had the skills to do both retail and rental housing, so this project was a joint venture of a major walkable urban apartment developer and a regional retail developer, a highly unusual team.

In essence the number of standard product types will have to change and possibly expand significantly. The high-density mixed-use office and housing over retail, such as West Village, will emerge as a conforming, standard product type. There is the "bury-the-box" mixed-use product type, which puts a big-box retailer in the center of a block surrounded with "liner" buildings. These liner buildings have retail on the ground floor and office or housing on the upper floors. The big-box store, movie

FIGURE 5.5. West Village was one of the pioneering mixed-use lifestyle retail centers with housing on the upper three floors when it opened in 2003. The structured parking is buried behind the buildings with only a small amount of teaser parking on the streets. (Source: Courtesy of Urban Partners)

theater, or urban entertainment arena is inward facing, opening to the sidewalk only at its front door. As shown in figure 5.6, the pedestrian walking by will be able to window-shop at the ground-floor retail, but will be oblivious to the fact that fourteen screens are showing movies forty-five feet away, just beyond the restaurant or clothing store she is passing on the sidewalk. Bury-the-box mixed-use development is one of the most important of the new evolving standard product types.

Beginning in 2005, many large homebuilders and commercial real estate investment trusts began to put their toe in the walkable urban water. The most prominent has been the New York Stock Exchange–listed homebuilder Toll Brothers, mentioned earlier. In a front-page story in the

FIGURE 5.6. The fourteen-screen Century Theatre was buried behind seven individually designed buildings, each with retail on the ground floor and offices on the upper two floors. The complex encompasses an entire block at the gateway into downtown Albuquerque and allows for continuous retail around all four sides of the block. (Source: Historic District Improvement Company)

Wall Street Journal in late 2006,[25] the headline screamed "Mr. Toll Turns to Towers; King of Suburban Minimansions Follows Boomers Back to the City; Catering to 'Hedge Fund Johnny.'" The company's chief executive officer, Bob Toll, feels that the downsizing and ever adventurous baby boomers and young, well-compensated Gen X-ers are fueling the move back to walkable urbanism. Yet it is still an exploratory step for the company; "I don't think you will see more than ten percent or fifteen percent shift gears and decide to move to the city," Mr. Toll said in the article. The hurdles faced by the earlier mixed-use developers, as outlined in chapter 3, have not gone away.

The Urban Land Institute goes much further than Bob Toll in their assessment of the future. In their annual projections of the future of real estate, entitled *Emerging Trends in Real Estate—2007*,[26] published jointly with the Big 4 accounting firm PricewaterhouseCoopers, they concluded that: "Far flung Greenfield homes may cost less, but filling the gas tank burns holes in wallets. Both empty nesters and their young adult offspring gravitate to live in more exciting and sophisticated 24-hour places—whether urban or suburban—with pedestrian-accessible retail, restaurants and offices. Transit-oriented development at subway and light rail stations almost cannot miss. New mixed-use town centers in the suburbs are also one of the hottest development trends."

Only ten years ago, the monthly magazine for the organization, *Urban Land,* primarily covered golf course communities and suburban office parks. Reading a 2007 copy of the magazine, sprinkled with phrases such as "sustainable development," "mixed-use walkable development," and "green building," one would get the impression that it was published by the Sierra Club or the Congress for the New Urbanism.

The online daily news site REBusiness Online recently reported that "developers are uniting this historically urban format with the increasingly popular 'live, work, play' motto of mixed-use development. [T]he newly evolved transit-oriented development trend is taking root in suburban areas across the country."[27]

These reflections by the Urban Land Institute and REBusiness Online underscore the trend toward walkable urbanism. There are still skeptics about the depth of the unmet market demand, the skill set of developers to build these complex places is certainly lacking, the legal zoning impediments are huge, Wall Street still has a problem trying to finance it, and drivable sub-urban product still gets significant subsidies. However, even with all of these obstacles, much walkable urban development is being built. Just think about how much will be built when these hurdles have been removed and the market can have what it wants.

6

DEFINING WALKABLE URBANISM

Why More Is Better

Architects and urban designers of the past century looked for *the* answer for the future of urban and metropolitan growth. From Frank Lloyd Wright and Le Corbusier and their promotion of what could be described as "drivable density," to Joel Kotkin and Robert Bruegmann, the current defenders for what I have been calling drivable sub-urbanism or sprawl, there has been a belief in a one size fits all—that the evolutionary history of urban growth has all been heading toward lower and lower density. In fact, there are only two general development patterns: drivable sub-urbanism and walkable urbanism.

In real estate circles, these development patterns are defined by density; by how much is built on a particular area of land. Real estate professionals measure density through "floor area ratio" (FAR),[1] which is the ratio of the amount of building (defined as heated/cooled space) to the amount of land on which the structure sits.[2] For example, if a 100,000-square-foot building is placed onto a 100,000-square-foot piece of land, it will have a FAR of 1.0. That building could be five stories high with each floor 20,000 feet square, or it could be one story and occupy the entire site; in both cases the FAR would be 1.0. Another example is 10,000 square feet of building on 100,000 square feet of land; the FAR is 0.10. This is regardless of whether it is five stories of 2,000 square feet per floor or one story of 10,000 square feet. Going the other direction toward higher densities, if the building is 1,000,000 square feet sitting on 100,000 square feet of land, the FAR is 10.0—a much higher density with at least ten stories of 100,000 square feet per floor.

Based on my experience in this country and in Europe, drivable sub-urban and walkable urban places are at two ends of the density spectrum: drivable sub-urban development tends to have a FAR between 0.005 and 0.3, and walkable urbanism's FAR tends to range between 0.8 and 40.0. The least dense walkable urban place is at least several times as dense as the most dense drivable sub-urban place.

Certainly more research needs to be done to refine these ranges, but the major point stands: there are only two fundamentally different ways of constructing the built environment in a market-viable manner. The broad variety inherent in these two patterns of development is discussed below, but in the end, the two represent stark alternatives, each with different implications for the future of growth in the United States.[3]

These two development patterns do not function in isolation. In fact, walkable urbanism and drivable sub-urbanism can be and almost always are immediately adjacent to one another. Witness the small-lot, single-family homes next to thriving downtown Birmingham, Michigan; a big-box power center right next to Reston Town Center, Virginia; and low-density neighborhoods a few blocks from downtown Palo Alto, California. The edge between drivable sub-urbanism and walkable urbanism is where the great battles over development will increasingly be fought as the demand for more walkable urbanism continues to change the character of the places where it can best be built. This conflict is in spite of the fact that low-density, suburban housing immediately adjacent to a walkable urban place potentially has the best of both worlds—suburban splendor within walking distance of a great place—but more on that later.

You'll notice that the two basic patterns leave out a third density range, from 0.3 to 0.8 FAR. This is an ill-fitting garment that is neither drivable sub-urban nor walkable urban. These places could be called "neverlands." Neverlands generally combine higher density residential with little in the way of street life. Most people have to rely on their cars for most trips from home. Neverlands were most famously promoted by the French, Swiss-born architect, Le Corbusier, who called for high-density buildings in park land, predominantly served by cars. His infamous 1922 Plan Voisin proposed tearing down the Left Bank of Paris for what he referred to as "rational" development, which was thankfully never implemented. However, his plan became the blueprint for most midtwentieth century U.S. public housing projects, such as Pruitt-Igoe in St. Louis and Cabrini Green in Chicago, which became symbols of blight and despair before they were unceremoniously torn down. Le Corbusier's vision of urban life is only partially to blame for the extreme social dysfunction of high-rise public housing in this country;[4] there are a very few examples of this vision that have worked and continue to work, such as middle-class Coop City in the Bronx and Park LeBrea in Los Angeles.[5]

Whether a mistake or a transitional phase, the neverland development pattern is not a long-term viable condition. It is neither "fish nor fowl." The market demand is going either to the far fringe for the newest version of drivable sub-urban development or to walkable urban places. Transitional never lands will either stay drivable density, thereby drifting downward in relevance and financial value, or will be retrofitted as walkable urban places, as will be discussed in chapter 7.

THE RANGE OF DRIVABLE SUB-URBAN POSSIBILITIES

The nineteen standard real estate product types discussed in chapter 3 represent much of the range of drivable sub-urbanism and are well known to most Americans. This development form is constrained by the need to keep density (FAR) low so as to:

- park cars at ground level,
- provide "terrestrial affiliation"—fulfillment of the desire for a piece of land to call your own, and
- provide the perception of privacy and prestige through space between buildings, especially for-sale residential.

For commercial developments in drivable sub-urban areas, this low density is especially driven by the need to park employees' and customers' cars. The typical car requires 300–350 square feet for parking and access lanes. In an office building the typical amount of square feet provided per worker is 150–200. In other words, more area must be provided for parking cars than for parking people.[6] This is typical of nearly all drivable sub-urban commercial development, whether office, hotel, or retail.

The cheapest way to provide parking is at-grade on an asphalt lot, which results in drivable sub-urban commercial development surrounded by fields of asphalt. This translates into a FAR of between 0.20 and 0.30 for the typical commercial sub-urban development—seventy to eighty percent asphalt and twenty to thirty percent building. Combine this with the need to move tremendous numbers of cars between the various commercial buildings and housing and you get four- to eight-lane roads in between the commercial buildings, just as Bel Geddes predicted in the Futurama exhibit.

The need for vast amounts of surface parking and wide roads to connect all the various uses in drivable sub-urban places is the major reason its density must be low. In my experience, the amount of land permanently dedicated to moving and parking cars in drivable sub-urban places is fifty to 100 times the amount of land permanently dedicated to pedestrians in a walkable urban place. This is a tremendous lever; a 50:1 lever demonstrates why transportation drives development patterns and why a place will be driven to one of these two development patterns.

THE RANGE OF WALKABLE URBAN PLACES

The range of densities, and therefore, characters available in walkable urban places is extremely wide, as the 0.8–40.0 FAR range indicates. Walkable urbanism as exhibited in Midtown Manhattan is at one extreme, and 1955 downtown Hill Valley is at the other extreme. The range in each place depends on the local market and political conditions.

Of course, high-density development with a particular FAR is not the only thing that has to be in place to make a walkable urban place work, as the late Jane Jacobs taught us all in her critically important *Life and Death of Great American Cities*. Having a rich mix of different uses—retail, educational, civic, hotel, office, and housing—is essential as well, as the term "urbanism" implies. The streets and sidewalks must also be safe and convenient and allow easy connections among these many uses. Running a major impediment, such as a freeway or large one-way streets, through the middle of great mixed density development will act as a barrier that no amount of density and varied uses can overcome.

There is one more concept that needs to be introduced to understand the range of possible walkable urban development. There are two levels at which both drivable sub-urbanism and walkable urbanism work: neigh-borhood-serving and regional-serving. Neighborhood-serving places consist predominantly of housing, as well as the commercial (retail and some office) and school buildings that support the housing. These places are relatively simple, because housing is more than eighty percent of the square footage; they are bedroom communities.

Regional-serving places are far more complex, anchored by uses that draw customers and employees from many miles away. These uses include urban entertainment (arenas, sports stadiums, destination restaurants, nightclubs, gaming casinos), culture (museums, performing arts centers), higher education, regional-serving office and industrial employment, and major civic functions (government offices, central libraries, convention centers). Regional-serving places can also include housing, which can provide a base of support for commercial and entertainment uses as well as eyes and ears on the street, which increase safety.

Many readers familiar with recent trends in the built environment will notice that I have not used some terms common over the past fifteen years, such as "transit-oriented development," "New Urbanism," and "traditional neighborhood development" (TND). The description "transit-oriented de-velopment" can and does apply to most regional-serving, walkable urban places. (It is possible, but not ideal, to be nontransit-served and still create walkable urbanism, as some of the examples below demonstrate). Transit-oriented development can occur in any density that supports transit.

In general, New Urbanism has played out on the ground as neighborhood-serving walkable urbanism. Its best-known, iconic projects, such as Seaside, Florida; Kentlands, Maryland; and Stapleton, Colorado,[7] are second-home or bedroom communities (neighborhood-serving) that may or may not become regional-serving someday. "TND" as a term tends to be interchangeable with "New Urbanism" and focuses on neighborhood-serving places.

New Urbanism and TNDs have played pivotal roles in the rebirth of neighborhood-serving places in suburban greenfields. Use of this type of development has demonstrated that walkable neighborhood demand can be built from scratch. Andres Duany, one of the founders of the Congress of the New Urbanism and a leading thinker and architect, has justified New Urbanism suburban development by saying that most future development will go to the suburban greenfield sites, so they might as well be walkable.

THE FIVE KINDS OF REGIONAL-SERVING WALKABLE URBAN PLACES

Based upon my recent experience throughout the country, there appear to be five kinds of regional-serving walkable urban places in U.S. metropolitan areas as of the mid-2000s. As the pent-up demand for walkable urbanism continues to be met, these places will form the building blocks of the growth of the country, both in our cities and in suburbs, because walkable urbanism will be built in both cities and suburbs. The five basic kinds of regional-serving walkable urbanism are (1) traditional downtown, (2) downtown-adjacent, (3) suburban town, (4) greenfield town, and (5) redeveloped regional and strip malls.

Traditional Downtown

Traditional downtowns have historically been the highest density place in the metropolitan area. High density is expected and not overly contentious when built in this kind of place. Based on my observations, an estimated two-thirds of the largest traditional downtowns in the country (metro areas of more than 1 million people) are reviving or have revived over the past fifteen years.[8] They are being built at FARs of between 4.0 and 30.0, though they seem to cluster in the 5.0–10.0 range. Recently reviving downtowns include San Diego; Portland, Oregon; Seattle; Denver; the Loop in Chicago (as opposed to the always healthy Gold Coast); Boston (as opposed to the always healthy Back Bay); Philadelphia (Rittenhouse Square/City Hall area and the Society Hill area); Baltimore; Washington, D.C.; downtown Manhattan (as opposed to the always healthy Midtown Manhattan); Orlando, Florida; and Milwaukee, Wisconsin. Even downtown Detroit is beginning to show signs of life.

Denver represents a typical reviving downtown; it is redeveloping at a FAR estimated between 5.0 and 7.0. Denver was hit by a massive economic recession in the mid-1980s, due to the collapse of energy markets, but by the early 1990s urban entertainment, hip lofts, and million-dollar townhouses were being built in the lower downtown (Lodo). When the new baseball stadium landed downtown in the mid-1990s, it added further excitement and complexity to the place. In 2004, Denver elected a novice politician as mayor. John Hickenlooper, who was a brewpub owner in Lodo, has further pushed the development of walkable urban places (figure 6.1) by garnering voter support for the most extensive light rail transit project currently under construction in the country. This revival, and most others, is home-grown and market-driven, has bipartisan political support, and only modest support from the federal government, which is still busy subsidizing drivable sub-urbanism. The new Denver light rail expansion has less than twenty percent federal investment; the rest is local tax funds. This split contrasts with the eighty to ninety percent federal share of road projects over the past few decades.[9]

Downtown-Adjacent

Although less dense than downtown, downtown-adjacent is still among the most complex kinds of walkable urban development possible. These

FIGURE 6.1. Strolling down the 16th Street Mall, a pedestrian street also served by frequent free shuttle buses, in the heart of revitalized downtown Denver. (Source: Stan Obert/Downtown Denver Partnership)

are places such as midtown Atlanta, West End in Washington, D.C., and West Philadelphia around the University of Pennsylvania. Universities are particularly good anchors for this kind of walkable urbanism, as midtown Detroit (Wayne State University); Cambridge, Massachusetts (MIT and

FIGURE 6.2. When built in the late nineteenth century, Dupont Circle was an elegant enclave of the well-to-do. Many of the original mansions were turned into embassies along "Embassy Row" in the 1920s and 1930s, but this did not halt the decline that occurred in the post-Second World War period. Dupont Circle revived in the 1980s, led by artists, gays, and students, to become one of the most culturally diverse and vibrant sections of Washington, D.C., at the turn of the twenty-first century.

Harvard); and Westwood (University of California-Los Angeles) in Los Angeles demonstrate. The range of FARs is from 2.0 to 10.0.

A particularly good example of a downtown-adjacent place is the Dupont Circle area of Washington, D.C. Twenty years ago, this section of town was considered very dangerous. After the pioneering investment by predominantly gay households, it has become one of the most hip and exciting places in the region. There is a significant concentration of residential and office space in Dupont Circle (figure 6.2), anchored by the largest embassy concentration in the world and think tanks such as the Brookings Institution and the Aspen Institute. The area includes more than 200 restaurants, from ethnic to white tablecloth; international, national, and local boutiques; more than fifteen small museums; thousands of rooms in hotels and small inns; and an entrance to one of the largest urban parks in the country, which is on Dupont Circle's border with Georgetown. The area is served by the Metro subway system, numerous bus routes, and Zip Car. The FAR is between 3.0 and 4.0 and will probably edge upward only marginally in the future due to building height limitations in the nation's capital and the area's historic designation.

Suburban Town

Numerous towns founded in the eighteenth and nineteenth centuries have been swept up in metropolitan sprawl and have found a new role in the lower to mid range of walkable urban density. When these towns were founded, everything had to be walkable, because the car had not been invented. As a result, they have "good bones," consisting of a grid layout of generally narrow streets, sidewalks, and a stock of older buildings. Overlooked for decades and most times run down from the 1960s into the 1990s, these towns became unique or upscale enclaves starting in the 1990s. The range of FARs tends to be between 1.0 and 5.0.

One unexpected example is downtown Birmingham, Michigan, north of Detroit (a.k.a. Motor City), which is not known for walkable urbanism. It has almost a hundred restaurants, moderate and high-end hotels, a major concentration of office space, and one of the two major concentrations of upscale boutique shopping in the Detroit region. There are many condominiums and apartments in the downtown, which is surrounded by very expensive, though small, single-family houses (known to realtors as "charming"). The FAR of downtown Birmingham is between 2.0 and 3.0.

There are hundreds of towns like Birmingham throughout the country, including Palo Alto, California, and most of the other towns on the peninsula south of San Francisco. Others examples include Pasadena and Santa Monica in the Los Angeles metro area; Redmond, Washington, east of Seattle, where Microsoft has its headquarters; Boulder, Colorado, northwest of Denver; University City outside St. Louis, Missouri; Evanston, Illinois, north of Chicago; and White Plains, north of New York City. Many of these towns got their start anchored by commuter rail service, such as the Main Line towns northwest of Philadelphia, or have recently been reconnected to a new rail transit system, such as Pasadena,[10] which now has two light rail stations in the exciting, walkable urban Old Pasadena.

Greenfield Town

A greenfield town springs up from virgin land, generally on the edge of the metropolitan area, where large enough land parcels are available. A greenfield walkable urban place requires that virtually everything required for urbanism, such as streets, sewers, traffic lights, and parks, as well as all of the buildings, has to be built from scratch—a massive undertaking. The best and oldest example of a greenfield walkable urban town is Reston Town Center, Virginia, which is on the highway to Dulles Airport northwest of Washington, D.C. The so-called "new town" of Reston, started in the 1960s by Robert E. Simon, was a typical drivable suburban place as it built out over its first three decades. The vast majority of the initial development was single-family homes and strip commercial. The major innovation was a trail system running through the huge development. Of course the trails were only for recreational purposes; they did not lead any place practical.[11]

Reston was taken over by Mobil Oil's land development division in the 1980s, and they began to envision a town center at the intersection of Reston Parkway and the Dulles Highway, a ±200-acre greenfield site that would look unlike anything developed from scratch in the U.S. postwar era until then. It consists of a Main Street with sidewalks and parallel parking on both sides of the street; the buildings come right up to the sidewalks. The parking decks, hidden from Main Street, supported the 770,000 square feet of office, hotel, and retail space developed in the first phase. When it opened in 1992, it immediately became a "place," achieving a critical mass of walkable urbanism, such that it became a favorite destination for western Fairfax County residents. For example, it became the best place in the area to take the kids to see Santa and to go ice skating. The second phase of 900,000 square feet of office space added by 1997 increased the walkability of the place. However, the addition of thousands of condominiums and rental apartments, as well as additional office and retail space, in the late 1990s and early part of the 2000s, confirmed Reston Town Center's role as a major regional-serving walkable urban place—what the current owner refers to as "a downtown for the twenty-first century." It has a FAR between 3.0 and 4.0, which is at the high end of the FAR range for most greenfield towns. The other unusual aspect of Reston Town Center (figure 6.3) is that it is not served by rail transit, though it does have bus service. It demonstrates that walkable urban development does not need transit to work. However, Reston also demonstrates the concept of being "transit-ready" due to its density and design. It will be connected to the regional Metro rail system by 2012. Transit planners would have been irresponsible if they had not made Reston Town Center a Metro station; being transit-ready is the best way to justify being connected to an eventual rail transit service.

One promising way to develop new greenfield towns is through the construction of lifestyle centers, initially viewed as another retail-only format, but now becoming a mixed-use format. As discussed in chapter 5, most of the newer projects are mixed-use and also include more extensive use of structured parking to support the increased density, including residential, hotel, and office. Most conventional, retail-only lifestyle centers were only 0.2–0.3 FAR. When mixed uses and structured parking are introduced, FARs can go above 0.8 and even get to 2.0.

As an executive of a moderate-sized private lifestyle center development company said in a retail trade magazine, "Consumers across the nation have gotten a sweet taste of mixed-use development and have a craving for more. There is a growing knee-jerk reaction to sprawling suburbia."[12] Interestingly, most of the development sponsors of these projects have been smaller, private firms, not the huge New York Stock Exchange–traded public firms, demonstrating the continued resistance by Wall Street to deviating from the nineteen standard product types. Wall Street's aversion to financing greenfield walkable urban development will certainly be swept away as the market becomes proven.

FIGURE 6.3. An aerial view of Reston Town Center in 2007 with high-rise offices, hotels, and residential buildings with ground-floor retail and parks. It was a greenfield vacant site in 1987 and has quickly become the new "downtown" for western Fairfax County, Virginia. (Source: Charlie Pruitt)

Redeveloped Regional and Strip Malls

Dr. Arthur C. Nelson of Virginia Tech has estimated that there could be 10,000 dead or dying retail centers (malls, power centers, and strip centers) in the country,[13] making them targets for redevelopment. Spurred on by the need for tax revenues, there is often significant interest from local governments in seeing the shuttered mall or strip center replaced by a tax-generating walkable urban alternative. Local residents understand that boarded up strip retail or a closed regional mall is bad for their community and property values.

The best recent example of a recycled failed mall is Belmar (figure 6.4) in Lakewood, Colorado, a middle-income suburb of Denver. The site was previously home to the Villa Italia regional mall, but it had closed, leaving only one department store open. The 103-acre site was cleared in 2003, except for that department store. In its place a twenty-two–block grid of

FIGURE 6.4. Belmar is the "new downtown" for the Denver suburb of Lakewood. This walkable urban development at build-out will include 1,300 residential units, a sixteen-screen movie theater, a Whole Foods Market, office space, and 175 stores. It replaced an abandoned 1960s mall. (Source: Continuum Partners, LLC)

streets and sidewalks was planned. The first phase of about 1 million square feet consists of retail, a multiplex theater, and housing and offices on top of the retail, as well as townhouses within a block of the main commercial streets. The FAR of the initial phase was 1.0–1.5. A Whole Foods market opened as part of the second phase in 2006. The infrastructure for the project was funded by nearly $200 million of city-backed bonds paid off by sales taxes generated by the new development. It was built by a privately owned New Urbanist development firm, Continuum Partners, LLC, and has been a market and tax-generating success from the day it opened in 2004.

Some of the best redevelopment of failed and failing malls and strip centers has been in Arlington, Virginia, in the Washington metro area. Arlington County had encouraged the building around the many Metro stations, starting when the transit system was first built in the 1970s. There were five regional-serving walkable urban places in Arlington County in 2007, which mainly took the place of obsolete strip retail originally built in the 1950s and 1960s. Arlington County leaders also pushed for the Metro system to be underground throughout most of its path through the county, which allows development to take place in a full circle around the station, not in just half of a circle, as happens when the tracks and station are aboveground, which can create "the other side of the tracks" phenomenon. Arlington County leaders also created walkable urban zoning around the stations to encourage walkable urbanism. This resulted in billions of dollars being invested in places such as Ballston, Pentagon City/Crystal City, Court House, Roslyn,[14] and Clarendon, most of which would have been lower middle-end development and maybe even slums otherwise. None other than the American Podiatric Medical Association declared Arlington "the best U.S. walking city"[15] in 2005. Of all people, foot doctors know about walkability.

Arlington in particular shows the potential of increasing density around rail transit stations in creating walkable urbanism. The majority of walkable urban places in the country have major rail transit connections, particularly subway, commuter rail, or light rail. Generally speaking, bus transit has neither adequate capacity nor the consumer appeal that rail transit has. Relying upon the car and bus, although possible, as Reston Town Center shows, is not optimal. There needs to be a diversity of transportation by which to get to a walkable urban place to help create the street life and support the retail, and that is best achieved by a rail system connecting the area to the rest of the metro region. A rail system also has more appeal to middle and upper-middle-class riders, and it shows investors the firm commitment of the government to a place, because it is difficult and expensive to move tracks once they have been laid.

It is possible to imagine other types of regional-serving walkable urban places emerging over time. More universities and even smaller colleges can use their presence to anchor a redevelopment of their neighborhood. Temple University in north Philadelphia and Franklin & Marshall in Lancaster are two examples of this, both in Pennsylvania.[16] It might also be possible for hospital complexes to anchor walkable urbanism, as is being most aggressively attempted around Johns Hopkins Medical Center in an extremely poor section of Baltimore and surrounding Lancaster General Hospital in Lancaster, Pennsylvania. Providing housing for doctors, nurses, and staff within walking distance, while encouraging medical offices and outpatient clinics and possibly retirement housing, will all spur a variety of retail and other commercial uses and housing.

NEIGHBORHOOD-SERVING WALKABLE URBANISM

In addition to these large, regional-serving walkable urban places, an extensive rebirth of local-serving walkable urban places is underway. This includes neighborhood-serving retail (grocery, drug and hardware stores, small restaurants, dry cleaners, etc.) supporting relatively high-density housing. This kind of neighborhood was very common before the 1960s, when local retail was killed off by suburban strip centers. However, as regional-serving walkable urban places emerge, these districts pop up like flowers in spring. Hundreds are emerging or redeveloping throughout the country, such as Larchmont Village and Los Feliz in Los Angeles, and Cleveland Park (figure 6.5) and Tenleytown in northwest Washington, D.C. Some of these have been hanging on for many decades, but saw an infusion of new life in the 1990s; others were nearly dead and vacant from the 1960s through the early 1990s, only to come back to life over the subsequent decade. Neighborhood-serving walkable urban places are the next spurt of walkable development following the establishment or redevelopment of regional-serving walkable urban places. Neighborhood-serving districts are natural adjuncts to regional-serving walkable places, providing the bedroom communities that support the regional-serving places.

It is important to point out that of the five types of regional-serving walkable urban places, three are predominantly outside the central city of the metropolitan area. Certainly the downtowns and downtown-adjacent walkable urban places took off first during the 1990s and have become the easiest walkable urban places to spot, given the high profile of a major downtown in a region. However, it is likely that fifty, sixty, or even seventy percent of all pent-up demand for walkable urbanism will be

FIGURE 6.5. Cleveland Park is an early twentieth-century walkable neighborhood that has become much more desirable since the opening of the Metro station in the late 1970s and the resulting revitalization of the commercial district along Connecticut Avenue.

satisfied in the suburbs. The suburban town centers, the greenfield towns, and the redevelopment of strip centers and malls will probably take the majority of the $30 trillion of development that Arthur Nelson forecasted will be built through 2025.[17]

TWO STARKLY DIFFERENT PREMISES: MORE IS LESS AND MORE IS BETTER

As we have seen, the differences between walkable urbanism and drivable sub-urbanism go beyond floor-area ratios. In fact, the two patterns of development have a fundamentally different premise by which they are designed, legally encouraged, financed, and built, and how they perform, for the developers, homeowners, investors, and government. The implications of these two premises are critical to how Americans invest their wealth, how local government is financed, and the various social, environmental, and foreign policy issues initially raised in chapter 4.

Drivable Sub-urbanism: More Is Less

Drivable sub-urban development reached a milestone on national TV when Lucy and Ricky Ricardo of *I Love Lucy* moved from New York City to the suburbs in a January 1957 episode. It was official. The American Dream was to be found only in the suburbs in low-density drivable sub-urbanism. The problem is that the Ricardos told their friends just how lovely their newfound paradise was, and their friends decided to join them. Fred and Ethel Mertz moved out of New York City to Westfield, Connecticut, on a subsequent *I Love Lucy* show in 1957. Many, many others followed.

The eventual result of all the Freds and Ethels moving to drivable sub-urban places was traffic congestion, despite constant highway construction and maintenance, increased pollution, and the inevitable decline of open space. This inspired the next generation in the 1980s and 1990s to move farther out to the expanding fringe. Yet the next generation of Freds and Ethels could not keep from telling their friends and coworkers how nice it was over the next development horizon. Thus, the cycle has continually repeated.

This continual outward thrust to grasp the suburban version of the American Dream began to demonstrate something no one could have guessed when people were floating over Futurama in 1939; as you build more drivable sub-urban development, you get less quality of life. In other worlds, *more is less*. The more that is built, the more the very qualities that attract the households to suburbia are degraded or destroyed, setting the stage for further development on the ever-expanding fringe. The American Dream based upon drivable sub-urbanism is elusive if growth is assumed to continue; the more you build, the more the promise is denied.

The rise of defensive, anti-growth neighborhood associations over the past two generations is a direct result of the more-is-less principle. In most cases, these associations formed in reaction to the threat of further drivable sub-urban development to the quality of life of existing residents. By the 1970s on, the development of a new strip mall or subdivision was met with growing opposition. The real estate developer who promised progress and quality of life from a new development was no longer trusted to deliver on that promise. Real estate developers were considered "town founders" in the early twentieth century, and had statues built to their memory and towns named after them. By the late twentieth century, the status of developers had sunk to be nearly the lowest of all professions; it seemed they had descended beneath the level of used car salesmen. Developers were the perfect villains in countless movies, such as *Who Framed Roger Rabbit, Sunshine State, Bladerunner,* and *Chinatown.* Because everything developers built degraded the quality of life for the existing residents, it has been easy for the public to buy this damning image.

The more-is-less premise also applies to the financial returns earned by owners of commercial real estate in the suburbs. Sprawl keeps on taking demand farther out, leaving owners with declining rents and higher vacancies. As a result, few in real estate investment want to own suburban property for very long, not trusting its mid- to long-term returns. Major institutions, such as pension funds and life insurance companies, held real estate assets for an average of about ten years a couple decades ago. Today, the period has dropped to five years, a sign that this historically long-term, forty-year asset has become a short-term asset. This is a sad sign given that so much of the country's wealth is tied up in the built environment, yet drivable sub-urban development has become more or less disposable; after millennia of being a long-term asset, this part of the built environment has become a short-term to mid-term asset.

Walkable Urbanism: More Is Better

When *Seinfeld* reached the height of its popularity during the mid-1990s, the turnaround of U.S. downtowns was just starting. Hollywood's extensive market research and the success of *Seinfeld* showed that this was a new trend, which encouraged a raft of television shows depicting the wide range of choices, excitement, and serendipity that walkable urbanism allows.

In walkable urban places, when more development and activities are added to the stew, more people are attracted to the street, thereby providing safety in numbers. The restaurants are more crowded, encouraging more restaurants and other retail, increasing rents, making buildings more valuable, raising property taxes, and on and on and on. In walkable urban places, *more is better.* Adding more density and uses makes life better and real estate values climb higher. It is an upward spiral of value creation. If a new housing development is built, this self-reenforcing spiral creates value for the entire district. Everyone benefits just by being within walking distance of the project, and the project is easier to rent by being close to the action. In the West End of Washington, D.C., a Trader Joe's food market opened on September 1, 2006. By October 1st, condominiums in the immediate area were using the selling point that you could "walk to Trader Joe's." These condominium developers did not pay Trader Joe's to move into the neighborhood, but it has certainly provided a financial benefit to landowners, developers, Trader Joe's, and the eventual buyers of the units. The more-is-better premise financially benefits the government tax rolls, because property and sales taxes go up. In revitalizing urban centers with a large population of lower income residents, the trend does have a serious negative consequence. Affordable housing and commercial space is squeezed out, a topic addressed in chapter 8.

The more-is-better premise is responsible for the revival of Washington, D.C.'s government finances. By the mid-1990s downtown Washington, D.C., was pretty much deserted; the district government was bankrupt and was taken over by the federal government. Then, in the late 1990s, downtown D.C. and the adjacent downtown areas began an amazing turnaround. By 2001, when the D.C. government was turned back over to the citizens, government finances were running a surplus; the downtown and downtown-adjacent revival were obvious to all. The district government's tax revenues went up more than thirteen percent annually from 2000 to 2006,[18] something no one would have forecasted when the federal government first assumed control.

The more-is-better premise means that property owners and the local government have a common interest in seeing the walkable urban place prosper. Bringing real estate investors together with local government is no small feat. The more-is-better premise gives private investors a reason to want services, such as cleanliness, safety, homeless services, event sponsorship, and affordable housing, to improve, and even encourages the private sector to pay for many of those improvements themselves. The more-is-better premise gives local politicians a reason to encourage walkable urban development, even if there has been tension between the political class and the real estate community.

The more-is-better premise has even resulted in examples of private real estate investors and corporations paying for and organizing reform efforts for the public school system, the last and most dreaded city government service to tackle. In reviving downtown Chattanooga, Tennessee, the private sector has paid for and built two new magnet elementary schools for the neighborhoods around downtown, which have become mixed-income, multiracial beacons of achievement. The Center City District, the private real estate–funded organization focused on downtown Philadelphia, is focusing attention and resources on the twenty-three public and charter schools serving the downtown and immediately adjacent neighborhoods. Known as the Center City Academic Region, the effort allows children to attend any school in the region that best fits them. The private sector (foundations and private companies) has been funding special programs and encouraging young families to stay in downtown as their children reach school age.[19]

The more-is-better premise can also change the dynamics of neighborhood relations. Not-in-my-backyard–oriented neighborhood groups (NIMBY), who many times are opponents of new development, now have a reason to modify their generally negative approach. If more development will improve the quality of life and real estate values of residences surrounding a walkable urban place, there may be a reason to encourage development. Of course, there are two kinds of neighborhoods—those that are down-and-out and would welcome change of any kind and those that are reasonably or very prosperous and are suspicious of change of any kind. Down-and-out downtowns and their surrounding neighborhoods easily see the more-is-better premise; anything is better than a deserted downtown or strip commercial. However, most of the market demand for walkable urbanism will probably take place in the inner suburbs of the favored quarter, places such as Ardmore, Pennsylvania, outside Philadelphia on the Main Line, and Westwood in the wealthy Brentwood section of Los Angeles. These neighborhood groups were trained on the drivable sub-urban-inspired, more-is-less premise and may be resistant to change of any kind.[20]

INFINITE CHARACTER OF WALKABLE URBANISM

One of the most important aspects of the more-is-better premise is that so many different types of activities can occur in a walkable urban place. Literally each street[21] is a building block of the place, and each can have a function, personality, and character all its own. The character can be that of urban entertainment with crowds on the street, neon lights, and activity until the wee hours of the morning. The character might be work-oriented with a sense of purpose and dignity. It might be a quiet, neighborly residential block; civic and grand to celebrate the common purpose of the town, city, state, or nation; or cultural or educational.

The best thing about a walkable urban place is that it can be all of these things, or just one or two of them, depending on the market. These different places can all be together, separated by a few hundred feet on different blocks yet within an easy walk of one another. In downtown Washington, there is the grandeur of the Mall and Pennsylvania Avenue with the monuments, the Smithsonian museums, the U.S. Capitol, and the White House adjacent to the revitalized urban entertainment streets with the new arena, restaurants, and nightlife adjacent to the stolid downtown office buildings for lawyers, banks, and lobbyists. There is also a growing, quieter residential district that goes to sleep early, just a couple blocks away. All of this diverse activity can be visited during a twenty-minute walk.

There will undoubtedly be conflicts as the premise of more is better plays out on the ground. The most common is the conflict between urban entertainment districts and residential districts. Just when the bars are getting heated up, the residences want to go to sleep, unless the patrons of the bars, generally younger people, also populate the residential districts. Noise from the bars, particularly at closing time around 2:00 a.m., is not what an empty nester couple in their 50s generally wants to hear. It is important to note that these are nice problems to have, problems of success, though they do have to be addressed and managed.

HOW WALKABLE URBANISM CHANGES A METROPOLITAN AREA

How many walkable urban regional centers will there be in a metropolitan area? It is too early to say because the trend is relatively new. However, as alluded to in chapter 5, the best place to see the future of metropolitan growth is in the Washington, D.C., metro area. Drivable sub-urbanism is very much in evidence on the fringe of the metropolitan area, but there are also more regional-serving walkable urban places than in any other metropolitan area in the country, and there is at least one example of each of the five types outlined above. Washington, D.C., is the new model of where the country is heading because it has the best of the new generation of subway systems. Since construction began in the 1970s, the Metro system has fundamentally changed how the metropolitan area works. The Metro system has been an unqualified success because of the elegant stations and cars, its safety, and the many jurisdictions that took advantage of the high-density walkable development potential around the stations.

Twenty years ago, there were two regional-serving walkable urban places in the region—Georgetown in D.C. and Old Town, Alexandria, Virginia—both relying upon tourism, based upon the historic fabric of these eighteenth-century towns. By the mid-2000s, there were seventeen regional-serving walkable urban places in the D.C. (figure 6.6) area, and five more seem to be emerging.[22] Of these seventeen, sixteen are built

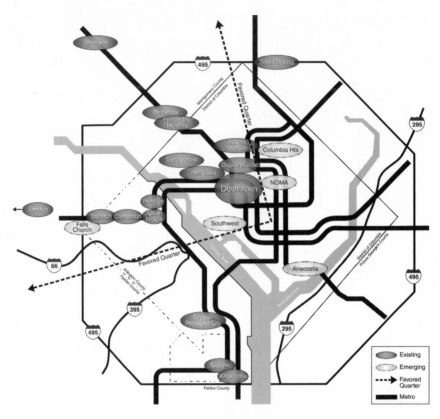

FIGURE 6.6. The Washington, D.C., metropolitan area is the new model of how the country is developing in the twenty-first century. This map shows where the seventeen existing regional-serving walkable urban places are as well as five of the emerging places. Notice that the bulk of the walkable urban places locate in the favored quarter.

around Metro stations, and the one without Metro service (Reston Town Center) will get a station by 2012. Significantly, downtown D.C. and the downtown-adjacent walkable urban places began to increase their market share of occupied office space in 2005, reversing a sixty-year downward trend. Downtown Washington is now the second healthiest office market in the country, after Midtown Manhattan.[23] No one would have predicted this as little as ten years ago.

The Washington region has about 5 million residents, which translates into about 300,000 people per regional-serving walkable urban place; this hints at the potential in other metropolitan areas. If the Detroit metro area, which also has about 5 million residents, has only four walkable urban places,[24] there may be a market for around thirteen to fifteen more. This market pressure is one of the reasons that downtown Detroit is reviving, despite having the worst image of any big city downtown and an economy that is going through a fundamental restructuring. In the face of these challenges, starting in 2004, the city of Detroit had more building permits than any municipality in the state for three years running. Almost all of that activity is in or near downtown; if anyone had guessed in 2003 that this would happen, they would have been mocked for even suggesting that it was possible.

MANDATE TO PROVIDE CHOICE

The two viable development options; low-density, drivable sub-urbanism and high-density walkable urbanism, provide the consumer with an amazing amount of choice. In a knowledge economy, this range of choice is not only possible, it is mandatory. No longer can just one choice, that is, drivable sub-urban development, be dictated, subsidized, and provided as the only option. Metropolitan areas that do not provide the choice the market wants are at a serious economic disadvantage. It would be like a grocery store offering only iceberg lettuce when the market also wants bibb, Chinese, romaine, batavian, lollo rosso, *and* iceberg. There is no one solution, nor should there be; the answer is both drivable sub-urbanism *and* walkable urbanism. Drivable sub-urbanism may be what some people want for all phases of their lives, and others may want a walkable urban place for all phases. In all probability, most will find that there are different ways of living in each phase of life. Having the choice available, without a government-mandated and subsidized, social engineering experiment, will level the playing field.

So the future is both drivable sub-urbanism *and* walkable urbanism, it's just that the pent-up demand over the next generation is for walkable urban. *All eyes to the future.*

7
UNINTENDED CONSEQUENCES
OF WALKABLE URBANISM

Any societal change produces unintended consequences, and this will be true of walkable urbanism as well. The three primary unintended consequences of walkable urbanism that can be understood so far are lack of affordable housing, a surplus of large-lot, single-family houses on the fringe, and the impact on independent stores and community character as national chain retailers move into the newly walkable places. More unintended consequences will certainly emerge as walkable urbanism expands.

LACK OF AFFORDABLE HOUSING

The greatest negative, unintended consequence of walkable urbanism is the lack of affordable housing. As the desire increases for walkable urban housing, many places are experiencing rapid gentrification. Gentrification has many positive aspects, including increasing the tax base; improving physical structures, amenities, and services; and initially creating mixed-income neighborhoods after years of being only lower income. However, many of these areas become largely unaffordable for middle and lower income residents. "Workforce housing" is needed for schoolteachers, grocery clerks, housecleaners, police, and other public employees, among others, as well as truly affordable housing for those households earning less income than the local-serving jobs provide.

The most common way for working families to find affordable housing in the drivable sub-urban world has been to "drive until you qualify." As discussed in chapter 4, if one is willing to drive farther to the fringe, and probably not in the favored quarter where most jobs now locate, the price of housing drops (actually the price of land under the house drops). This is one of the reasons drivable sub-urbanism has proliferated, and is often cited as a major benefit of sprawl.

The current dearth of walkable places has created a supply shortage that has pushed prices to extremes in most existing walkable urban places, reflected in the high sales price premiums discussed in chapter 5. Yet even as more walkable urban places are built, there is a natural governor on supply: walking distance. The area incorporated in a walkable urban place is by definition limited to walking distance; most regional-serving walkable urban places will be 200–500 acres in size. Naturally, transit extends the reach of workers whose jobs are located in a regional-serving walkable urban place; so a variation of "drive until you qualify" works here as well—that is, "ride until you qualify."

The problem is that it will take time to meet the pent-up demand for walkable urbanism; it is so overwhelming in most major cities that much of the housing in regional-serving walkable urban places is today at the top range of the metropolitan area and the housing near transit stops in walkable urban neighborhoods has also increased in value. The beginning of the next housing upturn will probably just make this situation much more difficult for lower income households.

Residents of many neighborhoods and some regional-serving walkable urban places bemoan the rising housing values that threaten to gentrify their community and change its character. Middle- and low-income residents of communities such as Silver Spring and Takoma Park, Maryland, just outside Washington, D.C., Harlem in Manhattan, Venice Beach in Los Angeles, and many university towns, such as Ann Arbor, Michigan, and Boulder, Colorado, have significant concerns about the lack of affordable housing. The fear of displacement of the poor grows as formerly obsolete, turn-of-the-century, well-built houses, industrial buildings, churches, and commercial buildings are reclaimed by the middle- and upper-middle-class. But the rise in market values cannot be stopped without destroying the wealth and freedom of U.S. society. This country is not going to embrace socialism or a command-and-control economy, nor should it, so the market will have its way. Walkable urban housing and commercial values will just continue to rise disproportionately over the next twenty years or so as the pent-up demand is worked down, so any solution has to accept this fact.

In the late 1980s, the federal government modified its approach to financing affordable housing by providing incentives for the private sector to build it. However, the federal low-income housing tax credit program (section 42) has a fifteen-year expiration, which means that the affordable rental units can be reverted to market rate in fifteen years. Another successful federal program, known as Hope VI, has provided high-density, walkable urban places for a mix of affordable housing and market-rate units. Many times, funds from this program have gone toward tearing down dense blocks of generally "neverland" public housing projects and creating new walkable urban communities, changing concentrations of poverty in "the projects" into mixed-income developments. The downside is that these Hope VI developments almost always provide fewer affordable housing units, although most housing agencies say they have successfully placed all their former low-income residents.[1] These two programs need additional funding at the federal and state levels. In addition, we need an expansion of the low-income housing tax credit program to broaden it to the next rung up the housing ladder—workforce housing for those making about average incomes but who still can not afford the average cost of housing, a common situation throughout the country.

Another form of affordable housing became available when drivable sub-urban development first grew in popularity in the 1950s and lower income families were able to live in "hand-me-down" older housing left behind. This old walkable urban product, generally built before 1930, became obsolete from a market perspective in the 1950s through the 1980s. Many well built buildings, such as mansions on Spring Garden Boulevard in north Philadelphia, high-end apartment buildings on Georgia Avenue in Washington, D.C., and substantial homes in the Adams section of Los Angeles near the University of Southern California, were written down in value significantly and often divided into low-income apartments. This option has all but disappeared due to gentrification.

In addressing the issue of affordable or workforce housing, it is important to understand that new production *must* be subsidized; the only question is by whom. Developers are faced with rapidly increasing construction costs, due to the inflationary pressure on construction materials due to demand from India and China, and the sharp rises in land prices driven by the demand for walkable urbanism. Therefore, developers are unlikely to provide any type of affordable housing if they are not offered attractive incentives or forced to do so by regulations. The latter situation basically pushes the subsidy onto the market-rate units the developers are building, which means that new buyers pay the subsidy.

Inclusionary Zoning

Many cities and counties are trying to meet the affordable housing crunch with inclusionary zoning policies, which mandate that any housing development over a set number of units must make some percentage of the housing, generally ten to twenty percent, affordable. The best example of inclusionary zoning is in Montgomery County, Maryland, a wealthy suburban county immediately adjacent to Washington, D.C., to the north in the favored quarter. Their inclusionary housing ordinance has been in place since 1974 and has resulted in the construction of nearly 12,000 affordable housing units through 2004.[2] It has generally been considered a success by local residents and by outside observers.

Inclusionary housing is a relatively painless way of providing affordable housing, because the cost of the required subsidy comes out of the underlying value of the land. By making it the law over a wide area that all housing projects must have a certain percentage of affordable housing, the required subsidy slightly reduces the value of the land in the entire area to which the law applies. Inclusionary zoning is in effect a hidden tax on land that subsidizes affordable housing, because land prices will be slightly lower to offset the lower value of the units being built for affordable housing. However, most landowners will not feel the reduction in land values, especially once the ordinance is in place and land values have adjusted to it. After the adjustment period, when land values may have dropped slightly, they will continue rising or falling, depending upon market conditions, just as if the inclusionary housing regulation was not in place. Therefore, inclusionary zoning is an easy and basic way to provide part of the answer to the affordability issue. The reason that it is only part of the answer is that just ten to twenty percent of new units is not enough to solve the problem.

Many places are adopting an inclusionary housing ordinance that sweetens the deal for developers for specific projects if they choose to build more affordable units than required in exchange for some benefit; for example, they are frequently allowed to build at a higher density.[3] New Jersey has adopted what it calls "growth share" housing. The state requires local jurisdictions to ensure that for every eight market-rate homes built, one affordable unit must be developed; it also requires one affordable housing unit for every twenty-five new jobs brought into the jurisdiction.[4]

The best potential way to encourage inclusionary housing ordinances throughout U.S. metropolitan areas is to link the issue to federal transportation spending, which is channeled into a metropolitan area through the state department of transportation and then through metropolitan planning organizations. If the federal transportation legislation, to be reauthorized next in 2009, would mandate that transportation funds from the federal government will be spent only in metropolitan areas with inclusionary zoning and other affordable housing programs, there would be a significant incentive to address this issue. This would be a major step both in addressing affordable housing and in providing an incentive not to invest in transportation infrastructure that encourages "drive until you qualify," taking pressure off the highway system as a benefit and justification.

Another important tactic to encourage affordable housing is permissive policies on granny flats and other accessory units. If homes were designed with a separate entrance leading to an "English basement" or unit(s) over the garage, accessible empty bedrooms could provide a vast inventory of rental affordable housing. Most jurisdictions make granny flats and accessory units illegal; this is another sign of fearfulness about people that are not "just like us" living in the neighborhood. There may be an average of at least one surplus bedroom per house in the country; this equals more than 100 million spare bedrooms that could be rented as affordable housing. The problem is that most of those bedrooms do not have a separate entrance. Allowing spare bedrooms to be built as an accessory unit in the future will be a major step toward providing affordable housing, while providing another source of income for home owners.[5]

Value Latching

Another powerful way to finance affordable housing is through "value latching." Walkable urban housing and commercial and retail space have been appreciating far faster than drivable sub-urban product, a reflection of the pent-up demand for walkable urbanism. This should continue, given the more-is-better premise discussed in chapter 6. These increasing values could be translated into financing for affordable housing.

Value latching allows governments or nonprofit agencies to latch on to rising property values to pay for the affordable housing. There are two types of value latching: direct or indirect. Direct value latching means that an investment, such as land or financing, could be made into a real estate project by government or a nonprofit agency. Rather than a financial return being made for that investment, a certain percentage of the new housing could be affordable housing. For example, government-owned land could be invested in a new housing project in exchange for the developer keeping a certain percentage of the units affordable in perpetuity.

Indirect value latching is more creative. If the government builds transit or overlays a new zoning district to encourage walkable urbanism, there could be mandated financial payments into an affordable housing fund if a private developer wants to develop in the area benefiting from these government actions. If there is a height limit in the jurisdiction, the air rights above the height limit are owned by the citizens of the municipality, and these air rights could be sold to pay for affordable housing or invested in a development project in exchange for affordable units. This obviously requires building over the height limit, which some people would fight to prevent. The impact on the viewshed from building higher must be balanced with the benefit of the funds the additional floors will provide for affordable housing.

The number of ways to finance affordable housing is nearly unlimited *if* you know where appreciating land values will be; it is precisely where the land is appreciating that there is a need for affordable housing—a perfect match. Government decisions on transportation and zoning help direct this growth. Techniques mentioned above, particularly value latching, use gentrification to pay for affordable housing.[6]

WHAT TO DO WITH OBSOLETE DRIVABLE SUB-URBAN HOUSING

As discussed in chapter 5, Arthur C. Nelson of Virginia Tech forecasted that owners of between 1 million (optimistic assumptions) and 22 million (probable) large-lot single-family homes in existence in 2000 will have a hard time finding buyers by 2025, due to changing demographics and development patterns outlined in this book.[7] Yet for now, drivable sub-urban development continues to be built due to legal codes, subsidies, financial standards, and developer know-how. Hundreds of thousands of McMansions have been built on large drivable sub-urban lots since 2000, and exurban population growth beyond the metropolitan fringe has been growing twice as fast as overall metropolitan growth.[8] As a result, the number of obsolete drivable sub-urban housing units on the fringe in 2025 may be even greater than Nelson is projecting. So what will happen with the millions of obsolete houses?

Learning lessons from our experiences during the 1960s through the 1980s, when the country shifted from walkable urbanism to drivable sub-urban development, there is certainly a high probability that large-lot single-family homes on the fringe might be broken up into apartments or condominiums or sold at bargain-basement prices to lower income families. This is not what homeowner associations, neighborhood groups, municipalities, and school districts on the fringe would want to see, so there would be considerable resistance. There was opposition to "block busting" in the 1960s as well, the practice of scaring generally white homeowners with the advice "sell now before more colored families move into the neighborhood." The resistance in the early twenty-first century to this kind of change will probably be even more substantial and well organized, due in part to the politically organized nature of the places where these houses are located. The owners of these fringe houses will take a substantial financial loss, just as those engaging in white flight from the cities did in the 1960s.

But there are other problems with the scenario of large homes being sold to lower income families or broken up into apartments. The first concerns the cost of energy. Let's assume that a gasoline-powered vehicle is the probable way to get to this housing in the near and midterm future and that the price of oil will continue to increase faster than inflation, due to both lower production (caused by declining supplies, dislocation due to terrorism, or manipulation by supplier nations) and higher worldwide demand. This will mean that lower income families occupying these then lower cost houses will have large gasoline bills. And the new tenants will have to heat huge houses that are "outstanding in their fields"—exposed on all sides to the weather, unlike more efficient apartments and townhouses in more urban settings.

Another problem is that today's homes, even high-end McMansions, are cheaply built in comparison to those grand houses and townhouses that were broken up into apartments half a century ago. Hollow doors and wall board are less durable than solid oak doors and lath and plaster walls. Many McMansions have been built with artificial components that do not have a proven track record of long life, such as plywood floors using glues that dry out over time and roofs that are built to last no more than ten years. The ultimate proof of the higher quality of the older grand houses and townhouses is that even after being broken up into rental apartments for thirty to sixty years—a very hard use of a property—many of these houses are being reconverted into single-family homes. These restored houses often use the same flooring, walls, doors, banisters, and slate roofs that were installed originally, sometimes 100 years earlier. Current construction standards are much lower, and it is doubtful the recently built houses will survive as long.

The country will be fundamentally restructuring how it constructs the built environment over the next few decades, trying to catch up with the pent-up demand for walkable urbanism. It appears that when the music stops, many families and investors on the fringe will be left without a market-viable seat. This change will become obvious when land prices as a percentage of the selling price for drivable sub-urban housing begin to flatten out and decline while walkable urban land continues to rise as a percentage of the house value. There will be fiscal pain on the metropolitan fringe for municipal and school district budgets, and maybe even bankruptcies, as a result of the pendulum swinging back toward walkable urbanism. Adjustments of this magnitude are never easy.

STARBUCKS VERSUS THE MOM-AND-POP COFFEE SHOP

A common complaint heard in revitalizing walkable urban places, particularly downtowns and downtown-adjacent places, concerns the influx of national and international retail chains. These are often the very chains that help make drivable sub-urban development so bland and uniform. The pioneers of the revitalization efforts are most times small, locally owned stores—retailers that might be called "funky." Just as the place becomes a truly vital retail location, the chains begin to move in.

Georgetown in Washington, D.C., was one of the few walkable urban places in the region in the 1980s. The retailing consisted almost entirely of locally owned places such as Commander Salamander (a teen clothing shop), Union Hardware (high-end draw pulls, latches, etc.), and Marvelous Market (high-end specialty food store). Over the past decade or so, national and international chains such as Restoration Hardware, Gap, and Smith & Hawkin, among many others, have joined the mix. The retailers are presently about fifty percent locally owned and fifty percent chains.

So is the invasion of chains a bad thing? First off, there are few legal mechanisms available to local government to do anything about it even if they want to. However, the infusion of chains, even big-box chains, is actually a good thing. It all depends on whether these chains bring unique products and services to the walkable urban place so residents do not have to leave the area, generally by car, to make a purchase. It is particularly good if the chain comes to the place in a walkable-friendly manner, not as a huge box set back from the street behind a surface parking lot. If instead the big box comes buried behind "liner" buildings of small shops, for example, it can make a very good neighbor and increase the vibrancy of the area.

National retailers probably control a majority of retailing in the contemporary world. They have taken multiple levels out of the retail distribution process, lowering prices and increasing selection. Many low- and middle-income families rely on big boxes in particular to stretch their budgets. Making the assumption that the consumer market is favorably disposed to big-box retailers, as shown by their patronage in the face of smaller retail options, the major issue is making sure the big box comes to a walkable urban place in a walkable urban manner.

There is still significant space for small, locally owned retailers, though they have only a minority of retailing today. Intensely neighborhood-oriented retailing, such as bakeries, which rely on freshness, nail and beauty salons, which in essence offer a form of personal therapy as well as a discretionary service, and many other retail categories are predominantly locally owned. Ethnic and high-end restaurants are the domain of local owners. There are very few national chains of high-end restaurants; it takes too much hands-on attention to detail and customer care for a constantly relocating, hired manager or chef of a national chain to deliver. Farmer's markets are also important locally owned retailing outlets; there were about 4,400 in the country in 2006, nearly double the number ten years earlier.[9]

National chains can also act very similarly to a locally owned retailer. An example of a national chain having a positive and sustained effect on a walkable urban place occurred in downtown Santa Fe, New Mexico. There are 650 stores within the intense walkable urbanism of Santa Fe's downtown. Only ten of these retailers are chains; the rest are mom and pops. These mom and pops include 200 art galleries, 150 restaurants, and many jewelry stores. Almost all of the locally owned stores cater to the huge tourist trade; locals need only so many concha belts. Around the Plaza, the heart of downtown, three stores have primarily catered to locals: Starbucks, Gap, and, until recently, Woolworth's. Certainly many of the customers of these three stores have been tourists, but at least half, and in the case of Woolworth's, possibly more, of the customers were local. The closing of the Woolworth's in 2001, when the entire chain closed, was much bemoaned. For many locals, particularly lower income Hispanic residents, it was the *only* locally focused retailer for them left on the Plaza. Woolworth's had "gone native" in its product offerings, the workers were all locals and had been there for years, and the "chili Frito pie" had been invented at Woolworth's on the Plaza and was a favorite food of locals for decades.

The issue is not whether an establishment is locally owned or a chain; it is whether the retailer addresses the sidewalk in a pedestrian-friendly manner, modifies its offerings to the local tastes, and brings more people to the streets. There is a valid concern that having *only* national retailers can make a walkable urban place lose its sense of uniqueness, just as has happened in countless strip malls and regional malls. This issue will be a particular problem for the greenfield walkable urban places, because each of these places will be developed by a single developer who is most comfortable leasing space to creditworthy national chains.

These developers can manage this, if there is the will to create a unique walkable urban place.

There will certainly be many other unintended consequences—potentially negative—of the pendulum swinging toward more walkable urbanism that can not be determined now. No social trend has only positive outcomes. One can only hope that the increasing financial values created by walkable urbanism, resulting in increased tax revenues for local governments, will be sufficient to address some of these unintended consequences.

8

ACHIEVING THE NEXT AMERICAN DREAM

Leveling the Playing Field and Implementing Walkable Urbanism

Dismantling the drivable sub-urban domestic policy in the United States is far more difficult to do than to say. The country had a recent discouraging experience with changing a fundamental aspect of everyday life—the failed attempt to join the rest of the world in using the metric system, throwing out the arbitrary, irrational English measurement "system."[1] This resistance to change in learning a new system certainly applies to planning, regulating, building, financing, and managing the built environment, which represents a third of the assets of the economy. Countless lessons have been learned about drivable sub-urban development that everyone involved with the built environment knows in and out—zoning codes, parking ratios, building single use projects, appropriate financing ratios, optimal densities for each real estate product, appraisal techniques, and on and on. All of these change with walkable urban development.

Drivable sub-urban development is simple: it is single-product–focused, all parking is inexpensively at grade, there are few conflicts between uses, everyone knows how to do it by now, financing is nearly automatic, and it is legally mandated. Developing walkable urbanism is a far more complex process, and moving to this development pattern will be far more difficult than converting to the metric system. To mix metaphors, it is comparable to learning to fly an airplane after knowing only how to drive a car; driving involves two dimensions while flying involves three.

Five general steps must be completed for the emergence of the next American Dream, walkable urban development. The first step is changing zoning and land-use regulations to allow walkable urbanism to be legal, generally through the use of "form-based codes" and "overlay" districts. The second step is educating the financial community about the unique financing issues and opportunities offered by walkable urban development, encouraging the built environment to be built for the long-term once again. The third step is ending the subsidies favoring drivable suburbanism, making sprawl pay its own way. The fourth step is investing in the appropriate infrastructure, particularly rail-based transit, because transportation drives development. The fifth step is intensively managing walkable urban districts to ensure that the needed complexity actually happens on the ground.

ZONING FOR WALKABLE URBANISM

The foundation of domestic policy is the law, particularly zoning laws and regulations. The current "Euclidean" zoning codes[2] were adopted by local governments in the early to mid-twentieth century to intentionally separate uses—to keep industrial activities and retail away from housing, rental housing away from for-sale housing, and hotels only near retail and offices. These zoning regulations generally outlaw mixed-use development, mandate setbacks from the property lines, require huge amounts of parking, put height limits on construction, and set many other requirements that practically allow only drivable sub-urban development. Once any basic set of laws, such as zoning, is put in place, it is very difficult to change, and it is now preventing the mix of uses needed for walkable urbanism.

Yet zoning *is* being changed in communities across the country. Many communities are now engaging new planning processes that ask local "stakeholders," who include property owners, neighbors, retailers, developers, and planning and elected officials, what they want to see in a defined walkable urban district. This includes much soul searching about what communities want to be "when they grow up." It is best if this soul-searching exercise includes market research to determine what is feasible; there is no reason to hope for luxury condominiums and high-end shops if there is no market for them.

Some places are developing form-based codes that are based not on the use, as most zoning codes are today, but on the form of the building. Most urban buildings can house a restaurant, a shop, an apartment—so long as the use addresses the sidewalk in a pedestrian-oriented manner. Pioneered by the Congress for the New Urbanism, form-based codes do not specify what goes on inside the building, making the assumption that the market is much better at figuring that out and it will change many times over the building's life.

In many cases these new form-based codes are being implemented through the creation of an overlay district, placed on top of traditional zoning maps, which makes it easier to develop according to these new codes. In other cases, the form-based codes in the overlay district completely replace the outdated zoning. The new district will be 200–500 acres in size, about two to four times the size of a regional mall, including its parking lots.

One example of where this has been done is downtown Albuquerque, New Mexico. Twenty-one standards were developed to take the place of the existing zoning; all promote walkable urbanism.[3] For example, the second of the twenty-one standards requires: "The front door of all buildings shall be visible from the street. If located more than 10 feet from the front building line, their [sic] location must be reinforced with additional graphics, lights, marquees or canopies." In addition, each standard includes a statement of intent (the statement of intent for principle two is, "Provide safe and easy passage from the public realm into individual buildings") and three pictures of actual buildings in downtown, one with an X through it and the other two as models of what is intended. When an application is made to develop a new project in downtown, the planning department evaluates whether the project meets these twenty-one standards, and if it does, the building permit is provided within three weeks.

Many other overlay zones have been created throughout the United States. They have allowed construction of places such as Reston Town Center, Virginia, and the redevelopment of Belmar in Lakewood, Colorado, but, as discussed in chapter 7, there is no better example than in Arlington, Virginia. The many walkable urban places in Arlington County, following the building of the Metro subway system in the 1970s, were all further sparked by overlay districts. Over the past thirty years, the county commissioners have encouraged citizens and property owners to craft overlay districts that are between 1,500 and 2,000 feet in radius from the various Metro stations. Each one of these places has its own character. For example, Clarendon has an overlay district, updated in 2006, that the *Washington Post* said would keep it "quirkier, cozier and build more green space."[4] The character of Clarendon has been evolving to be more residential and restaurant-oriented. Less than a mile away to the west of Clarendon is the Ballston district, anchored by another Metro station (figure 8.1). The district includes an urban regional mall, headquarters for corporations and national trade associations, midrise rental and for-sale housing, retirement housing, hotels, and urban parks. Although physically close together, these two walkable urban places have completely different market orientations and unique characteristics.

Redeveloping Obsolete Strips and Neverlands

As referred to in chapter 6, there is a movement to use overlay zones to redevelop obsolete commercial strips, creating walkable urban places. As sprawling suburban development has continued to move to the fringe, the obsolete commercial strips left behind decline in value, attract lower-end users, and many times are completely abandoned. There are huge swaths of dying or dead strip commercial development throughout the country,

FIGURE 8.1. Arlington County, Virginia, demonstrated that the combination of transit and a walkable urban overlay zone results in impressive urbanism. One example is Ballston, which has been transformed from obsolete strip commercial and car dealers into millions of square feet of high-density office, hotel, residential, and retail development over the past twenty-five years, all within walking distance of the Metro station.

where most of the 10,000 declining or abandoned strip retail centers are located, as mentioned in chapter 6.[5] The closer to the downtown these obsolete strip commercial areas are, the more likely they will be redeveloped. The closer-in strip commercial sections tend to have older, better quality buildings, narrower streets, and more generous sidewalks because they were laid out in the nineteenth and early twentieth centuries before society began pandering to the needs of the car. As these streets continue out from downtown to the suburbs, they generally become so wide that they form complete pedestrian barriers. The streets then act as dividers, not as connectors, of the two sides, making it more difficult to redevelop them.

One of the many examples of strip commercial in the country is Memorial Drive, which heads east from downtown Atlanta for fourteen miles until it ends at Stone Mountain. The entire history of retail since 1920 is on display along this street. Close to downtown, Memorial Drive is a two-lane road with a turning lane and parking on both sides; about five miles out, it becomes a 1950s four-lane road with no parking on the side of the street, where one of the first regional malls in the Atlanta area was built in the early 1960s (now mostly abandoned). The next section of Memorial Drive grows to four lanes with a median down the middle, a turning lane, and no parking on the sides of the street. This section is flanked by 1970s and 1980s strip retail, auto repair shops, and cheap motels. The final section of Memorial Drive, closest to Stone Mountain, is six lanes wide and has turning lanes and no parking on the sides of the street. It is flanked by big-box retailers, grocery store–anchored strip centers, and new car dealers. It is the tamer, more pedestrian-oriented section near downtown that has been revitalizing in the 2000s. The 1960s through 1980s strip retail is all deteriorating, creating problems and loss of value for the surrounding residential neighborhoods. The 1990s and 2000s strip commercial is healthy as of 2007, but who knows about the future. Every metropolitan area in the country has multiple examples of Memorial Drive—a cancerous, use-it and throw-it away form of the drivable sub-urban built environment.

We are beginning to reclaim these commercial strips. The success of the downtown Albuquerque overlay zone, described above, led directly to the East Downtown (EDO) overlay zone in Albuquerque, adopted in 2004.[6] It focused on generally obsolete retail and office space along both sides of two major streets leading into downtown. The EDO district was defined as just one lot deep from both sides of both streets; attempting to extend the energy from the redeveloping downtown to this immediately adjacent commercial district. A reviving Victorian residential community was immediately adjacent on all sides, and special attention was made to ensure that the neighborhood was protected. The anchor for EDO was the abandoned 1917 Albuquerque High School at the intersection of these two

FIGURE 8.2. Old Main at the Lofts at Albuquerque High is a rental apartment conversion of this much beloved 1917 building. This project, which also includes for-sale lofts, retail, and office space, anchors the EDO corridor just east of revitalizing downtown Albuquerque. Its revitalization is partially explained by the overlay zoning for the Central Avenue corridor, adopted by City Council in 2004. (Source: Rob Dickinson, Paradigm & Company)

major commercial streets, which was redeveloped in 2002 into rental and for-sale lofts and a restaurant (figure 8.2). The further development of new retail with housing above along with the redevelopment of older, transitional retail originally built in the 1920s all began to occur immediately following passage of the EDO overlay zone. EDO is a pioneering model in the redevelopment of strip corridors in the country.

Neverlands Redevelopment

There are two other important types of more recently developed neverlands that hold the potential for transformation into walkable urbanism. The first of these is the initial car-driven places, built primarily in the 1950s, before the full flower of drivable sub-urbanism emerged. As first discussed in chapter 2, developers took baby steps away from 1955 downtown Hill Valley in the 1950s by setting the buildings back just a little from the street to allow one or two rows of parking with additional parking in the back. Examples include Nob Hill in Albuquerque; the initial Garfinkle's "suburban" department store location in Tenleytown in northwest Washington, D.C.; Suburban Square in Ardmore, Pennsylvania, outside Philadelphia on the Main Line; Park Cities in Dallas; and Lake Avenue in Pasadena, all built in the 1950s and early 1960s. First developed as an evolutionary step toward car-friendliness, these places have found new life by stepping back toward pedestrian-friendliness. They have reemerged from the doldrums they had sometimes sunk into during the prime of suburban development in the 1970s through the 1990s. In many cases they have revived to become major centers of walkable urbanism, encouraging the surrounding housing to be rehabilitated. In addition to the original quasi-walkable urban design of these places, they tend to benefit from being in the inner-suburban areas of the favored quarter.

The eight blocks known as Cary Town in Richmond, Virginia, went from being the location of the suburban "carriage trade" before the Depression up until the 1950s, including one front-parking-lot strip center (with only two rows of parking, so the stores are relatively close to the street with additional parking in the back), to a depressed, nearly abandoned commercial area between the 1970s and early 1990s. This decline also depressed the housing values nearby. During the mid-1990s, the place began to emerge as the alternative, hip boutique and restaurant location for the region. The one-screen movie theater in Cary Town has been purchased and rehabilitated by a nonprofit organization and now runs independent films. The surrounding housing values have gone up tremendously, and on most nights, the sidewalks are bustling with people of all ages.

The second transitional type of neverland, and the type that will pose the biggest challenges over the next ten to twenty years, is the initial edge cities such as Tyson's Corner, outside Washington, D.C.; King of Prussia, outside Philadelphia; South Coast Plaza in Orange County, California; the Galleria in Dallas; Post Oak in Houston; Troy, north of Detroit;

Perimeter Center in Atlanta, and many others. The focus of much 1970s and 1980s commercial development in this country, these areas have become "neither fish nor fowl," because they have greater than suburban density but zero walkability. The floor area ratio (FAR—the ratio of the amount of heated/cooled space in a building to the amount of land on which the structure sits) of these places is between 0.5 and 0.8, neither drivable sub-urbanism nor walkable urbanism. These former edge cities were the ultimate fulfillment of Le Corbusier's failed vision, many times combining high-rise offices and hotels, the huge one- to two-story regional mall(s), and sometimes some isolated high-rise residential space, all separated by six- to eight-lane highways and freeways that make them completely unwalkable. All of these places are located on major super-highways, but few have rail transit.

Over the next couple decades, these places will be a major focus of much higher density development. They will probably get overlay zoning and transit connections to the rest of the region, bus and trolley circulator systems, and perhaps narrower roadways that are suitable for walkable urban development.[7] Perimeter Center did get a heavy rail station in the late 1990s, although it has not yet had a noticeable effect on the urban design of the place. Tyson's Corner will get four Metro stations in 2012, but it is locally acknowledged that the transition to walkable urbanism will be difficult and made more so by the Metro line and stations probably being located aboveground, which will mean walkable development will take place on only half of the area near the station, with the other half being "on the wrong side of the tracks."

A model of how this transition can happen is the Dadeland area of Miami. This transitional neverland is home to 2.6 million square feet of office space, a big-box retail center, and Dadeland Mall, the most profitable mall in the Simon Company national chain. As of 2000, it was completely unwalkable in spite of a FAR approaching 1.0 and the presence of a new heavy rail Metro line and two stations, providing a transit connection to downtown Miami. A master plan for the future redevelopment of the Dadeland district was prepared by Dover Koll, New Urbanism planners, that mandated walkable urbanism, taking the form of midrise buildings up to the sidewalks, retail on the ground floor, and either housing or office space above. As a result of the plan and enabling legislation, including new form-based codes passed by Dade County Board of Commissioners, the surface parking lots across the street from the Dadeland Mall have since begun to see the development of numerous walkable urban projects that are changing the character of the place.

The future of the regional malls anchoring these former edge cities will be played out in their surrounding surface parking lots. With the cooperation of the major tenants, these parking lots could be converted into high-density housing and commercial uses, parking decks could be built, and rail transit could provide another option to get to the mall. With these changes, the regional mall produces a whole new category of walkable urban places to add to the five mentioned in chapter 6. A good example of this walkable urban future for regional malls is Valencia Town Center, about thirty-one miles northwest of downtown Los Angeles. The very conventional Valencia regional mall has an appendage—an outdoor "Main Street" development that comes right up to the food court entrance to the mall. The six-block-long Main Street contains restaurants, movie theaters, and boutiques with offices and housing on the upper floors. This Main Street has become the true heart of the area.

Unfortunately, many buildings in these edge city neverlands are owned by companies financed by Wall Street. As Bob Larson, the prominent real estate investment banker, said, "These mixed-use walkable projects are being done by small companies; the investment community will not allow national companies to do that yet." The Wall Street investors will figure it out soon enough, but as of 2007, they are watching and waiting to see how the demand for walkable urbanism will play out. The current political and real estate leadership in these edge cities may not see the walkable urban future, working under the assumption that "if it ain't broke, don't fix it." It takes great foresight to see a change as large as the shift from drivable sub-urbanism to walkable urbanism, and many will not see it or choose to ignore it.

FINANCING WALKABLE URBANISM

The built environment financial world, now ruled by Wall Street–inspired underwriting standards, as mentioned above, is slow in understanding the emerging reality of walkable urbanism. A combination of lack of experience with this type of development and the blinders of current methods of evaluating real estate investments makes this a significant institutional barrier. Yet financial markets will have to adjust because the market demand and the growing experience of primarily smaller and mid-sized developers will require it. In addition, many national homebuilders have added separate divisions since 2005 to build walkable urban projects; this is one of the ways Wall Street will learn to modify its approach.

The key reason major financial institutions will change is that few assets provide long-term cash flow like real estate and the built environment does. This allows financial managers to line up the long-term cash flow *needs* of pension funds, life insurance policies, and retirement funds with long-term cash flow *sources,* which walkable urbanism offers. Currently, most financial institutions with long-term cash flow needs rely on the spinning of short-term investing repeated over time.

One of the missing elements of financing a long-term asset such as real estate or infrastructure is patient equity.[8] Because equity invested in a real estate project is at much greater risk, the expected return is much higher than the interest charged for the debt in the project. Therefore, most equity is anything but patient, because it is so expensive. Drivable sub-urban development, with its nineteen standard product types, has evolved to require as little equity in the project as possible and return that equity as fast as possible. The result of this approach is the constant pressure to "value engineer" the cost of construction down and not build long-term, well built projects, especially because sprawl will probably just move the demand for the apartment project, neighborhood center, or hotel farther to the fringe in ten years or so. There is little reason to build well built projects because the current system of measuring financial returns cannot see beyond years seven to ten; why build expensively when the benefits cannot be measured?

Walkable urban projects are more costly, as mentioned earlier. This is due to inherently more expensive multiple-story construction, better expected finishes, and increased marketing risks, among other reasons. As a result, the construction budget must be generally twenty to forty percent higher than for drivable sub-urban projects, as is the cost of land. The result is that more equity must be invested, but the project will not be able to retire that equity quickly, as in conventionally financed projects. This means that most of that new equity must be patient—a very rare but required commodity.[9]

Financial institutions need to learn the lessons that many old real estate families have known for centuries: the need to invest patient equity to maximize mid- and long-term cash flows. The Grosvenor family in Great Britain, the owner of much of the land in the West End of London for the past 300 years, and the major old line New York City real estate families, such as the Rose family, have built and owned key walkable urban projects for decades and have built some of the most secure family fortunes of all time. However, these are private fortunes that are highly secretive; there is no thirty-year-old Wall Street analyst studying their growth and success. Instead, these analysts are comparing real estate returns to all other asset classes—Standard & Poor's 500, the Dow Jones Industrial Average, etc.—on a monthly and quarterly basis, hardly the benchmark that real estate should use.

Yet the size of the demand for walkable urbanism and the many examples now on the ground should eventually comfort Wall Street in understanding and financing these investments. In addition, many much larger private sources of investment funds are available today, many investing in large infrastructure projects, such as the purchase of toll roads and airports, as well as long-term real estate projects. Many of these funds do not have to be measured by Wall Street analysts, so they are free of the short-term measurement constraints Wall Street imposes. Stephen Ross, the chief executive officer of the privately held Related Companies, one of the largest developers in the country, has said, "The best way to finance real estate is to stay private, not go public on Wall Street; it provides the flexibility real estate demands."[10]

ENDING THE SUBSIDIES FOR DRIVABLE SUB-URBAN DEVELOPMENT

An important part of leveling the playing field for walkable urbanism will involve changing the way local governments offset the costs of infrastructure for new development, as outlined in earlier chapters. Generally, governments have used an unpredictable "extractions" process, in which a deal is cut between a developer and the local municipality. The developer pays for something the town or city needs, whether or not that improvement has anything to do with the proposed development. This approach leads to much uncertainty for the developer and investors and has a high potential for corruption.

Many state and local jurisdictions are now using more straightforward "impact fees" to ensure that new developments help pay for the municipal services required by the development. Impact fees are based upon formulas that anyone can understand before a development process begins. They outline how much each kind of project will pay for infrastructure costs that directly and indirectly result from the project's development.

However, if impact fees are the same for both high-density walkable urbanism and low-density drivable product, the high-density product is subsidizing the low-density product because costs for low-density drivable sub-urban development are so much higher on a per-unit basis. As mentioned above, a fiscal analysis of four of the ten categories of infrastructure in the city of Albuquerque, New Mexico, discovered that the cost of fringe infrastructure was twenty-two times higher per housing unit than the cost for in-town residential development. For these four infrastructure categories, a drivable sub-urban house cost $22,000 per unit, while an in-fill high-density house cost $1,000 per unit. A $22,000 impact fee was considered too large of a differential to impose on fringe development, so the City

Council approved impact fees eleven times greater for each new house on the fringe compared to new in-town housing—$11,000 for fringe development versus $1,000 for in-town. This resulted in a scream of outrage from the development industry that was heard in the state capital in Santa Fe. At the next state legislative session in 2005, the real estate industry very nearly got the state to mandate that impact fees must be the same everywhere within a municipal jurisdiction, which would have made it legally binding that in-town housing permanently subsidize fringe development's infrastructure needs. The measure was defeated on the last day of the legislative session, but the development industry will certainly try again.

Others are taking a more aggressive approach in encouraging development that puts the least strain on public resources. Illinois is giving businesses an edge if they choose locations that are served by transit and close to affordable housing for their employees, to try to offset the ease and public cost of fringe development.[11] The Illinois Business Location Efficiency Act of 2006 increased corporate income tax credits offered under the Economic Development for a Growing Economy (EDGE) program by ten percent for such efficient locations. Companies in areas that don't qualify can up their EDGE credits by creating a remediation plan that may offer employer-assisted housing, shuttle services, pretax transit cards, or carpooling assistance.

INVESTING IN WALKABLE URBAN INFRASTRUCTURE

As explained in chapter 1, transportation drives development. This means that public investment in the rail transit system in particular is crucial to encouraging walkable urbanism. For example, the major reason the Washington, D.C., region has emerged as the model of future metropolitan development is the transformative power of transit investments. These spurred the even more substantial real estate development that has emerged around numerous transit stations. The billions of dollars of real estate development around Ballston, Court House, Friendship Heights, Columbia Heights, Dupont Circle, Silver Spring, Carlyle Square, etc., would not have occurred without *first* building the transit line and the station. The same principle applies to highway transportation spending; commercial real estate development is at the freeway on- and off-ramps, but that development comes *after* the highways and the on- and off-ramps are built.

A major national source of funding for transportation is the federal transportation bill, which is reauthorized every six years. The revenue comes primarily from the eighteen-cent-per-gallon federal gas tax drivers pay at the pump; monies are used to fund the federal portion of transportation spending on highways and transit. The federal transportation bill is the largest domestic discretionary spending bill in the annual budget; its roots go back to the 1956 commitment to build the Interstate Highway System. The current version is known as SAFETEA-LU—the Safe, Accountable, Flexible, Efficient Transportation Equity Act: A Legacy for Users. Even though the law was significantly revamped in 1991 in recognition of the completion of the interstate highway construction era, this spending has remained heavily weighted toward highways. SAFETEA-LU guarantees spending of $286.4 billion dollars over six years, with only about fifteen percent—$45.3 billion—guaranteed for transit.[12] The overall bill grew by thirty-eight percent over the last iteration, but that did not result in a significant shift to transit and walkable alternatives. The vast majority of the funds still go to programs aimed at traditional highway projects.[13]

Most of the transportation funds allocated through the law are transferred from federal coffers to the state departments of transportation (DOTs); the funding is viewed as simply a return to the states of the gas taxes paid by the state's drivers. Most state DOTs still see their mission as building high-speed roads, a la the interstate. The losers in this system have been metropolitan areas, which have direct control over only a small portion of this money,[14] even though they are home to the vast majority of the population.[15]

Transit systems lose too, because although the states have the freedom to allocate a good portion of these transportation funds for transit projects (called "flexing" in transportation parlance), most are unlikely to do so, no matter how dire the need.[16] In addition, although the federal match rate is technically the same for road and transit projects (eighty percent federal, twenty percent local), the designated pool for funding new transit projects is so low and the demand is so large that in practice most have received only about fifty percent federal funding, and shepherds of these projects must jump through far more regulatory hoops than road projects.

However, there is some hope. Beginning in 1991, each subsequent federal transportation law has gradually expanded the scope of federal transportation spending, allocating special funds to improve air quality, provide for bicycling and walking facilities, and help communities co-ordinate transportation and land-use planning.[17] Savvy state and local governments are taking advantage of these new programs. Encouragingly, SAFETEA-LU makes $4.5 billion available for projects specifically to im-prove bicycling and walking,[18] a huge increase over the $2 million avail-able in 1991 (yet still just 1.5 percent of the total in the bill).

To encourage walkable urban development in the future, a substantial shift has to take place in federal, state, and local transportation spending, starting with the reauthorization of the federal transportation act in 2009. Only minimal new highway construction on the fringes should be under-taken, because the demand for walkable urbanism is so great that we are going to have a difficult time keeping up with it, much less building roads to the fringe that will be viewed as obsolete in the not so distant future. The continued spending on highway-oriented infrastructure in the early twenty-first century will look silly from the perspective of 2020. Much of the infrastructure built on the fringe of metropolitan areas will be con-sidered wasted investment. Instead, transportation funding should shift to fixing the transportation infrastructure we already have and diversify-ing transportation investments that support walkable urbanism—tran-sit, bicycling, and walking. A few states, most notably New Jersey,[19] have shifted their transportation spending priorities in this way.[20] But given the history and priorities of most state DOTs, the most effective way to move toward more appropriate transportation investments would be to give the metropolitan areas[21] more power over the purse strings, and to make a higher percentage of the federal transportation dollars flexible—open to use for more than roads.

Although federal dollars are important and help drive the priorities set locally, they account for only about twenty-five percent of the total surface transportation spending; states and local governments provide the rest. For now, with the difficulty in shifting federal transportation spending priorities, many places have turned to local funding sources and have found that residents support transit. For example, the Regional Transit District in the Denver area built and opened a "starter" light rail system in 1996 with thirty-five miles of track, focused on the rapidly reviving downtown. In 2004, the new mayor, John Hickenlooper, supported a sales tax proposal to expand the system, while also supporting more road infrastructure. The voters approved a $4.7 billion, twelve-year bond measure to create an expanded system[22] that will be the largest new transit system in the country since the Metro in Washington, D.C. The bond will fund the addition of another 119 miles of light rail track, eighteen miles of bus rapid transit, and fifty-seven new stations. Planning is ongoing for the areas around most of the proposed stations for walkable urban development at a density and scale seen only in downtown until now. Over eighty percent of the funding for this $4.7 billion expansion has been raised locally; the federal portion is less than twenty percent. All across the country, voters are approving transit ballot measures; since 2000 the success rate for such measures has been about seventy percent,[23] directing more than $100 billion to new transit projects. Denver's example shows that although federal transportation spending is important, taking local control is possible and probably required, at least until federal transportation policy can be revamped.

The American bias against transit must be overcome. The notion that transit is an old-fashioned transportation option meant only for the poor is dangerous and threatens the country's economic prosperity and the environment. Transit is in fact a public service and a public good that increases choice, spurs economic development, and gives us an important tool in the fight against climate change. Europe, China, and Japan invest significantly more than the United States in transit and will be in a much better position to prosper economically in light of probable higher energy prices while contributing to the solution for climate change. Funding priorities can change; Denver has recently shown the way.

The complexity of creating walkable urbanism has resulted in the emergence of new entities to develop the strategy for and manage these places. These entities typically take the form of nonprofit business improvement districts (BIDs), which raise operating revenues by property owners voluntarily raising their property taxes, generally by five to ten percent. More than 1,200 BIDs exist in the United States and Canada, and they are now an accepted prerequisite in the successful redevelopment of traditional downtowns.[24] Some walkable urban places, particularly greenfield development such as lifestyle centers, have for-profit management. The lifestyle center is generally owned by a few companies and many times only one. Some private-sector service companies, already managing stadiums, arenas, and convention centers, are considering entering the business of managing walkable urban places. They might be hired by the BID board to outsource management.

The strategy and management of a walkable urban place starts with the definition of its geography. Drawing a boundary between the walkable urban place and the surrounding drivable sub-urban development is crucial to mollify the probable opposition by the residents of the suburban neighborhoods to the continued growth of the walkable place. Design and management tactics can keep some of the unintended consequences of vital walkable urban places (e.g., noise, parking overflow, cut-through traffic) from creeping into the suburban neighborhoods.

The BID management function starts with a definition of which services the city government will provide—the baseline, such as police coverage, trash removal, street sweeping, and public parking. Additional services provided by the BID on top of the baseline might include:

- increased levels of cleanliness—more than the city can provide—including power-washing of the sidewalks, more garbage cans, and continual litter pickup;

- improved safety through "ambassadors" roving the streets, including reporting disturbances to the police via special radio connection, assisting the homeless in finding services, and providing directions;
- creation, management, and/or promotion of entertainment throughout the year to keep visitors coming to the district, such as holiday events, outdoor concerts, and recruitment of buskers (people who provide live performances for tips); and
- development of a visitor signage program—also called "way finding"—to help drivers and pedestrians find popular destinations.

The management functions of BIDs can expand to include taking over the parking strategy for the walkable urban place, which can include visitor directional signage for the various parking lots, a common validation system, improved shared use of the parking, and building more parking.

The management of walkable urban places can expand into the real estate development business, including:

- land assembly to encourage new development,
- providing "gap financing" for new development or redevelopment, such as providing the patient equity mentioned above,
- joint venturing with private developers on new projects, and
- developing the initial projects in a reviving place to demonstrate to the private development community that there is a market for a particular type of product.

After having success in redeveloping a downtown, some BIDs and other walkable urban place managers are now taking on even larger challenges. RiverCity Partners in downtown Chattanooga, Tennessee, has been developing a river walk along the Tennessee River and was involved with the privately funded Tennessee Aquarium in downtown, the world's largest freshwater facility. The Center City District, the BID for downtown Philadelphia, is attempting to attract more business to downtown and has floated more than $40 million of bonds for infrastructure improvements.

The success of walkable urbanism and the management organizations responsible for that success have not been free of criticism. BIDs are effectively a new form of government. The head of a BID is basically the "mayor" of the walkable urban place, something the actual mayor may not be happy with, because of jealousy or having his or her presumed electoral prerogative taken over. In one of the nastiest battles, the common head of the three large BIDs in Manhattan, Dan Biederman, had a painful run-in with Mayor Rudolph Giuliani in the late 1990s. Biederman's three BIDs included Bryant Park, which most observers feel is the most successful urban park in the country under his leadership; the redevelopment of Grand Central Station and the surrounding neighborhood; and the resuscitation of the 34th Street commercial district, where the major department stores stayed in town, in contrast to virtually every other city in the country. Biederman did an outstanding job in every respect, except one: Giuliani wanted the credit. The mayor took Biederman on publicly and after dragging him through the mud, forced him to drop one of the areas for which he was responsible.

The controversy pointed out the reality that these management organizations can lack political legitimacy. No matter how good a job they do, they are supported financially and are responsible to property owners, not the voters. It is important for these organizations to have a continuous outreach program to citizens, the mayor, and city council. Otherwise, a political price will be paid, much time will be wasted, and progress may even be stalled. In downtown Albuquerque, New Mexico, Mayor Jim Baca started the revitalization of downtown. The next mayor was less supportive of downtown revitalization, because he had significant support from suburban developers, so the redevelopment went into a stall. It is crucial to have political support for a downtown revitalization process until it reaches "critical mass,"[25] because it is rather fragile until then.

There are also concerns about the government shirking its responsibility to the private sector, although this is generally not a real issue if the public baseline service level is set fairly. The level of service needed for a downtown or other walkable urban place to compete with regional malls, for example, is much higher than any city can afford to provide alone, so the area businesses must assume responsibility. The improved level of service for downtown or other walkable urban place may spurn a backlash in the neighborhoods of a city; every city has a downtown/neighborhood competition for resources. But this can be diffused through education of neighborhood activists, because almost all walkable urban places create financial surpluses for the municipality, so they subsidize residential neighborhoods. Downtown Philadelphia, for example, is four percent of the land mass of the city, but provides more than sixty percent of the tax revenues while consuming far less than that in city services.

Whatever the management structure selected—nonprofit BID, for-profit management, or some combination—it is crucial to think both strategically about where the place is heading and about managing the day-to-day to make sure it gets there. Local political leaders should embrace these organizations as the ultimate economic development generators for the city. All the fancy economic development strategies, such as developing a biomedical cluster, an aerospace cluster, or whatever the current economic development "flavor of the month" might be, do not hold a candle to the power of a great walkable urban place. Place-based strategies that create walkable urbanism will attract the broad spectrum of talent required to build a great and vibrant economy. Build a great place, offering the choice of many ways of living, including all kinds of drivable sub-urban and walkable urban options, and they will come—the young entrepreneurs, the venture capitalists, the skilled technicians, and the schoolteachers. If only drivable sub-urban living is offered, the metropolitan area is nothing but an undifferentiated commodity. Offering drivable sub-urban product plus many different kinds of walkable urbanism is the way to broaden the appeal of the region, its economy, and its tax base, not to mention the richness of its quality of life. It seems that the country may be divided into two types of metropolitan areas in the future: those that offer choice in development patterns, especially great walkable urbanism, and are growing faster than the gross domestic product, and those that offer only drivable sub-urban develop. The latter may be economically left behind in the future.

Much has to be done to level the playing field and encourage the emergence of more walkable urbanism. Making it legal by changing zoning and other regulations; changing government subsidies to more realistically charge for the costs of drivable sub-urban development; and redirecting infrastructure investments to walkable urban districts, particularly rail transit, will all help transform the domestic policy of the past half century. A national and local debate must address appropriate transportation infrastructure needs, particularly for the 2009 reauthorization of the federal transportation bill. But these changes are just the beginning. The need to reeducate the developers, planners, architects, and public officials about this new animal—walkable urbanism—is critical. The financial community needs to understand the differences in providing the capital, particularly the need for patient equity, for this kind of development rather than drivable sub-urban product. Finally, strategic planning and management of walkable urban places is required for their ultimate success. This laundry list might appear pretty discouraging. But one can take heart in knowing that many places throughout the country are well on their way to making these changes; there are many successful models from which to learn.

WHAT IF WE DO NOT HAVE ENOUGH TIME?

After the subsidies and legal straitjacket encouraging drivable sub-urbanism are removed and when the development and finance industries figure out how to deliver this kind of development, a richer variety of walkable urban places will undoubtedly become more available in more locations. The development industry in particular is filled with creative people who know how to deliver homes, office space, and parks, and many are eager to try these new approaches. They will respond to the need in ways that are impossible to guess.

However, even if the playing field is leveled, it will take a considerable amount of time to satisfy all of the pent-up demand. If thirty to forty percent of households want walkable urbanism and an additional thirty percent are not certain what they want or are willing to accept either kind of development, this means upward of half or more of U.S. households want or will accept something other than drivable sub-urban development. As mentioned earlier, newer places such as Phoenix, Atlanta, and Los Angeles probably have much less than ten percent of their housing stock in a walkable urban condition. In older places such as Boston, Chicago, and even Washington, D.C., probably no more than twenty-five percent of the housing stock is in a walkable urban condition. New real estate and infrastructure is added only at the rate of about 2.0 percent of the built environment per year, as discussed in chapter 5.[26] The significant pent-up demand will probably be unsatisfied for decades, especially considering how difficult it will be to remove the subsidies and change the laws prescribing drivable sub-urbanism.

In the best of all possible worlds, the market would just naturally adjust to this new demand. With the subsidies and legal restraints eased, the distortions to the market will be eliminated and the Futurama social experiment will come to an end. But what happens if conditions converge that require a more rapid shift to walkable urbanism? Two looming issues may force the hand of government and industry: climate change and energy costs.

Dr. James Hansen, the leading climate scientist at the National Aeronautics and Space Administration, said in 2007 to the *New York Times*, "We only have 10 years until a tipping point is reached when the earth will go down a path that will make the planet a fundamentally different place."[27] If Dr. Hansen turns out to be correct, do we have time for the market to correct on its own? Nearly seventy-five percent of CO_2 emissions result from the built environment (buildings and transportation), and we know that walkable urbanism produces less CO_2 and other greenhouse gas emissions than drivable sub-urban development. So it might be necessary to promote walkable urbanism as part of the solution to climate change.

Likewise, what happens if political leaders of the country decide that the economic and political price of imported oil has become too high?

Or if oil prices rise significantly as peak oil is reached? It may become essential to create a built environment where most buildings are higher density, more compact, and therefore more energy-efficient, and where people can reduce their need to buy expensive gasoline by taking more day-to-day trips by foot, bicycle, or transit. A shift away from our current energy consumption patterns would be possible only if such a shift were made in the built environment.

TILTING THE PLAYING FIELD TOWARD WALKABLE URBANISM

If these scenarios come to pass, a new domestic policy may have to be put in place to not just level the playing field, but promote walkable urbanism in much the same way that the current domestic policy promotes drivable sub-urban development. Yet proceeding with subsidies is dangerous because the economic assumptions used by business will adjust to those subsidies, distorting the market, just as the market has been distorted for the past half century toward drivable sub-urbanism. These subsidies and policies are difficult to retire once the reason for their existence fades, because large industries adjust their economic models to them, supporting politicians who support the continuation of the subsidies. However, policy makers might deem the urgency of addressing climate change and oil dependency as justification for subsidies for the development of sustainable walkable urbanism. One way of addressing the permanence of the policy is by having a "sunset" provision that will roll back the walkable urban policies at a certain date, say after ten years.

An important means of promoting walkable urbanism is to designate regional-serving walkable urban places in the metropolitan area. These districts would probably be around existing transit stations or in locations that are or could be transit-ready. Using Washington, D.C., as a model, where there is now one regional-serving walkable urban district for every 300,000 people, which is probably a conservative estimate of the demand, a metropolitan area of, say, 1.2 million would designate four such districts, with the central city downtown being one of the four. Each district would be between 200 and 500 acres in size, within walking distance from an existing or planned transit station or stations serving the district. Nationally, there were 233 million people living in metropolitan areas, which would mean that there is a need for about 800 regional-serving walkable places in the 361 metropolitan areas as of 2005.[28] There are probably far less than half that number today, and most of those existing today are far from their build-out potential in population or jobs.

Another means of tilting the playing field is to provide government assistance in developing the overlay zoning for a walkable urban area. The state or federal government could provide planning incentive grant money to local governments to do the required research, seek community input, and hire the urban planning consultants to create these walkable urban places. This work needs to be done before the private development and finance industry will be attracted to these districts. Very few developers are interested in spending their money and time planning a district, and it is the responsibility of the local government to determine their future land use.

Another way of favoring walkable urbanism would be to subsidize its infrastructure, making the assumption that there are societal benefits to more compact development. Policy could dictate that the costs for infrastructure, such as transit, highway, water, and sewer, would be provided by the government to those developers and their customers who build in the designated walkable urban districts.

Probably the best way of encouraging walkable urbanism is through transportation investment. Transportation priorities should shift toward transit and maintenance of existing roads rather than the expansion of existing roads or the building of new ones, starting with the 2009 reauthorization of the federal transportation bill.

Because the federal transportation bill is primarily funded by gasoline taxes, the increased spending on transit would mean that drivable sub-urban transportation would be subsidizing walkable urban transportation. A parallel is the subsidy of health care programs by taxes on cigarettes. The public came to accept this arrangement over a very few number of years; the same could happen regarding gas taxes paying for transit. For example, the money for a highly successful new streetcar line built in downtown Portland, Oregon, in the early 2000s was paid by government bonds, serviced by parking revenues—rather poetic. However, one never knows when huge issues such as climate change, peak oil, and kicking foreign oil addiction will be raised in the public debate. The 2009 reauthorization of the federal transportation act will be a major bellwether of how seriously the country will take the need to make such a transformation.

THE MORAL IMPERATIVE TO BUILD WALKABLE URBANISM

This book has focused on a variety of market, fiscal, economic, foreign policy, and social equity reasons for allowing walkable urbanism to compete and even thrive. There may come to be a moral imperative to build walkable urban places. Development of mixed-use walkable places may be a significant, if not the most important, element in reducing greenhouse gas emissions. In addition, walkable urbanism will certainly lessen dependence on oil, potentially reducing dependence on foreign suppliers. Walkable urbanism will build wealth for the residents and property owners, revive or continue the economic growth by providing increased densities in existing communities, and take pressure off land consumption on the fringe of the metropolitan areas. Walkable urbanism can potentially provide affordable housing from the wealth created, if local governments and citizens choose to make that a priority.

The ultimate irony is that Manhattanites, who live at 800 times the average U.S. density, have the smallest "ecological footprint" per person in the nation and have the most expensive real estate prices (by the absolute dollar as well as on a price-per-square-foot basis) of any place in the country. These issues are connected. Many Washingtonians, Santa Feans, Portlanders, and a growing number of people throughout the country want to enjoy the pleasures and opportunities of walkable urbanism; luckily, this is environmentally responsible and people are willing to pay a significant premium to do so.[29]

Walkable urban development is already a growing part of the American built environment, in spite of the legal, financial, and other obstacles. It will even become part of the *next* American Dream over the next generation. The only question is whether the market will just take its course over many decades or whether walkable urbanism will be part of new American domestic policy to speed up the process. Either way it is coming—*all eyes to the future.*

Notes

INTRODUCTION

1. United Nations Population Division, "World Population Prospects: The 2006 Revision Population Database," http://esa.un.org/unpp/index.asp ?panel=1. Accessed January 2007.
2. The Census says, "The general concept of a metropolitan area is that of a large population nucleus, together with adjacent communities having a high degree of social and economic integration with that core." Metropolitan areas have a population of more than 50,000.
3. "Exurbia" is defined by Merriam-Webster Dictionary as "a region or settlement that lies outside a city and usually beyond its suburbs and that often is inhabited chiefly by well-to-do families."
4. U.S. Census and Allan Berube, Audrey Singer, Jill Wilson, and William Frey, "Finding Exurbia: America's Fast-Growing Communities at the Metropolitan Fringe," The Brookings Institution Metropolitan Policy program, Washington, D.C., 2006.
5. Stephen Roulac, Roulac Global Places, LLC—primary research for this book.
6. For Philadelphia, see http://www.centercityphila.org/docs/SOCC06_Residential.pdf. For Detroit, see http://www.brookings.edu/metro/umi/pubs/20061025_downtowndetroitinfocus.pdf.

CHAPTER 1

1. Susan B. Carter and others, eds., *Historical Statistics of the United States,* (New York: Cambridge University Press, 2006), 2-82, 2-83; David R.

Weir, "A Century of U.S. Unemployment, 1890–1990: Revised Estimates and Evidence for Stabilization," *Research in Economic History,* 14 (1992): Table D3, 341–343.

2. U.S. Department of Labor, Bureau of Labor Statistics, "Labor Force Statistics from the Current Population Survey," http://data.bls.gov/data/home.htm

3. Expo2000, "The History of World Expositions," http://www.expo2000.de/expo2000/geschichte/detail.php?wa_id=14&lang=1&s_typ=5.

4. New York in 1939–1940 was the peak of the world's fair movement; never again would more people attend one. The need for international exhibitions has been met by permanent "world's fairs" and amusement parks, such as EPCOT and Disney World, art biennials, and the Olympics.

5. General Motors, Futurama brochure from the 1930–1940 New York World's Fair, 1939.

6. David Gelernter, *1939, The Lost World of the Fair* (New York, NY: Free Press, 1995), p. 25.

7. Estimates by author after decreasing attendance for repeat and international visitors as compared to the population of the country in 1940.

8. Joseph J. Corn and Brian Horrigan, *Yesterday's Tomorrows: Past Visions of the American Future* (Baltimore, Md.: Johns Hopkins University Press, 1996).

9. Bel Geddes dedicated the book "To the fifty million Americans of the generation of our grandchildren to whom all that is written here will be commonplace." Those grandchildren are the postwar Baby Boom generation.

10. Norman Bel Geddes, *Magic Motorways* (New York: Random House, 1940). My copy of *Magic Motorways* is inscribed "To Jack in recollection of a tough job we did together, Norman, 14 March 1940." Jack is John Dineen, the General Motors manager of the Futurama exhibit.

11. E. B. White, "One Man's Meat," *Harper's Magazine,* July 1939.

12. Lewis Mumford, "The Skyline in Flushing," *The New Yorker,* July 29, 1939.

13. Bel Geddes, *Magic Motorways.*

14. American Studies at the University of Virginia, "America in the 1930s: 1939 NY World's Fair," University of Virginia, http://xroads.virginia.edu/~1930s/DISPLAY/39wf/taketour.htm.

15. Brendan Nee, "Fair and Square: The Planning Legacy of World's Fairs," http://www.bnee.com/research/fair-and-square-the-planning-legacy-of-worlds-fairs/.

16. Construction, "New Residential Construction Index," U.S. Census Bureau, December 2006, http://www.census.gov/const/startsan.pdf.

17. Ibid.

18. As a reprise, GM tried to replicate the impact of Futurama by sponsoring Futurama II at the 1964 New York World's Fair, offering a "Jetsons" view of the future this time. The 1964 version had minimal impact on society because the original Futurama vision was alive and well and had years to continue unfolding.

19. Kenneth T. Jackson, *Crabgrass Frontier: The Suburbanization of the United States* (New York: Oxford University Press, 1985), 15.

20. Cal Jillson, *Pursuing the American Dream: Opportunity and Exclusion over Four Centuries* (Lawrence, Ks.: University Press of Kansas, 2004).

21. Kenneth T. Jackson, *Crabgrass Frontier*.

22. U.S. Census, December 2006.

23. Charles Glaab, *A History of Urban America*, (New York: Macmillan, 1983).

24. U.S. Census Bureau, Census 1920.

25. Carter et al., *Historical Statistics of the United States*, 2-110; Stanley Lebergott, *The Americans: An Economic Record* (New York: W.W. Norton, 1984), 66; Thomas Weiss, "U.S. Labor Force Estimates and Economic Growth," in *American Economic Growth and Standards of Living before the Civil War*, ed. Robert E. Gallman and John Joseph Wallis (Chicago: University of Chicago Press, 1992), 22; Thomas Weiss, "Long-term Changes in U.S. Agricultural Output per Worker, 1800–1900," *The Economic History Review* 46, no. 2 (1993): 324–341.

26. Bureau of Economic Analysis, Bureau of Labor Statistics, and Gross Domestic Product by Industry Accounts. December, 2006.

27. These industries, led by the automotive industry, fall into the category of businesses and jobs economists refer to as "export" or "base" jobs. Export industries are responsible for the infusion of new revenue into a metropolitan economy, and they are the primary reason a metropolitan area exists. They contain the highest paying jobs in the economy and give the metropolitan area its basic character. Export jobs produce a ripple factor that stimulates the other two kinds of businesses and jobs: regional-serving and local-serving. Generally speaking, for every export job, two to three regional- and local-serving jobs are created. (The reverse is also true; when an export job is lost, two to three support jobs will also be lost). Export jobs generally represent about a third of all jobs in the metropolitan area, the rest being regional-serving jobs (e.g.,

lawyers, bankers, hospital workers, construction workers) and local-serving jobs (e.g., grocery clerks, police, teachers). No study has looked at all components of the automobile industry as broadly defined here, including not just the production of cars but the raw materials, finance, insurance, dealers, service, road building, etc. In all probability, the broadly defined automotive industry accounted for ten percent of all American jobs at its peak in 1970, which means that about a third of all export jobs were affiliated with the industry, using a two-fold ripple factor (two required on local-security jobs for every one export job). Conservatively, about a third of all jobs in the country would be directly or indirectly supported by the automobile industry in 1970.

28. Michael Southworth and Eran Ben-Joseph, *Streets and the Shaping of Towns and Cities* (Washington, D.C.: Island Press, 2003), 79; Daniel Solomon, *Global City Blues* (Washington, D.C.: Island Press, 2003).

29. Jackson, *Crabgrass Frontier,* 208.

30. Carter et al., *Historical Statistics of the United States,* 4-533; 1939–1985: Economic Report of the President (1987), Tables B-70, B-71.

31. Mortgage insurance is the equivalent to having your parents cosign for you. It makes the difference between whether the bank will make the loan or not, and it lowers the interest rate by one to four percentage points, dramatically lowering the monthly payment and allowing many more families to qualify.

32. Jonathan Levine, *Zoned Out: Regulation, Markets, and Choices in Transportation and Metropolitan Land Use* (Washington, D.C.: Resources for the Future, 2006).

33. Minnesota Department of Transportation, "Mn/DOT Celebrates Interstate Highway System's 50th Anniversary," http://www.dot.state.mn.us/interstate50/50facts.html.

34. Tom Lewis, *Divided Highways: Building the Interstate Highways, Transforming American Life* (New York: Viking, 1997).

35. Constance E. Beaumont and Elizabeth G. Pianca, "Why Johnny Can't Walk to School: Historic Neighborhood Schools in the Age of Sprawl" (Washington, D.C.: National Trust for Historic Preservation, 2002), 15.

36. The author was driving behind a school bus in an Atlanta suburb one early morning in the 1990s. The bus stopped in front of a house, where a little girl boarded. The bus then started moving again and immediately turned left into a school that was directly across the street from the girl's house. Upon calling the school district, I found out that 100 percent of

all children had to be bused to school, because it was considered too dangerous for anyone to walk.

CHAPTER 2

1. Although there are fifteen categories of infrastructure, such as water, sewer, telephone, drainage, etc., transportation is by far the most important in shaping the built environment. The only infrastructure category in urban history that was as important as transportation was perimeter defensive walls from the beginning of urban civilization through the Renaissance. The walls directly defined the size and density of cities. With the rise of the nation-state and the internal security provided by this new form of government, city walls were no longer needed. Many of these walls were torn down to be replaced by ring roads.

2. Andrea Cattaneo, Economic Research Service, U.S. Department of Agriculture, "Balancing Conservation Costs and Benefits," *Amber Waves* 1, no. 4 (2003), http://www.ers.usda.gov/AmberWaves/September03/pdf/findingsresourceenvironmentsept2003.pdf.

3. U.S. Census Bureau, American Community Survey 2004; Alan Pisarski, *Commuting in America: A National Report on Commuting Patterns and Trends* (Westport, Conn.: Eno Foundation for Transportation, 1987).

4. U.S. Census Bureau, U.S. Department of Commerce, "Value of Construction Put in Place," Washington, D.C., 2007.

5. Construction, "New Residential Construction Index," U.S. Census Bureau, December 2006. http://www.census.gov/const/startsan.pdf.

6. Ibid.

7. Being one of the seven largest metro areas in the country, Philadelphia also has smaller, secondary favored quarters with high-end housing concentrations—one north of the city toward Bucks County and the other east toward Cherry Hill, New Jersey.

8. Co/Star data for office statistics and RCLCo research, using U.S. Census data, for location of high-end housing concentrations.

9. The abstract from a famous 2001 study by Miller McPherson, Lynn Smith-Lovin, and James M. Cook starts with the following: "Similarity breeds connection. This principle—the homophily principle—structures network ties of every type, including marriage, friendship, work, advice, support, information transfer, exchange, co-membership, and other types of relationship. The result is that people's personal networks

are homogeneous with regard to many sociodemographic, behavioral, and intrapersonal characteristics. Homophily limits people's social worlds in a way that has powerful implications for the information they receive, the attitudes they form, and the interactions they experience. Homophily in race and ethnicity creates the strongest divides in our personal environments, with age, religion, education, occupation, and gender following in roughly that order. Geographic propinquity, families, organizations, and isomorphic positions in social systems all create contexts in which homophilous relations form." Miller McPherson, Lynn Smith-Lovin, and James M. Cook, "Birds of a Feather: Homophily in Social Networks," *Annual Review of Sociology* 27 (August 2001): 415–444.

10. David Brooks, *On Paradise Drive: How We Live Now (and Always Have) in the Future Tense* (New York: Simon & Schuster, 2004), 69.

11. Myron Orfield, *Metropolitics: A Regional Agenda for Community and Stability* (Washington, D.C.: Brookings Institution Press; Cambridge, MA: Lincoln Institute of Land Policy, 1997).

12. This was in spite of a Presidential Executive Order by Carter, which was later reissued by Clinton, that encouraged agencies to locate downtown.

CHAPTER 3

1. The Hoyt Group, "Real Estate Capital Flows Research Program," http://www.hoyt.org/capital_flows/index.html.

2. Timothy Curry and Lynn Shibut, "The Cost of the Savings and Loan Crisis," *FDIC Banking Review,* 2002 http://www.fdic.gov/bank/analytical/banking/2000dec/brv13n2_2.pdf.

3. Ibid.

4. See the U.S. Department of Transportation, Federal Highway Administration, "TEA-21—Transportation Equity Act for the 21st Century," http://www.fhwa.dot.gov/tea21/suminves.htm#fl.

5. There is much truth to this accusation. Many real estate developers purchased S&Ls in the 1980s and then turned around and made loans to their own projects, having the S&L take on massive risk, which was government-insured. In addition, many S&L owners continually refinanced loans at ever higher appraised valuations, justifying larger and larger loans. This was a Ponzi scheme with federal loan insurance

backing it up, leading to inevitable bankruptcy, the government holding the bag. Only a few S&L owners, most infamously Charles Keating, went to jail.

6. Japan had a comparable financial sector crisis at about the same time; banks had made a huge number of loans to real estate projects that then went sour. However, the Japanese did not recognize the problem or do anything drastic about it, like the U.S. did with the Resolution Trust Corporation (RTC). This was probably due to the Japanese desire to not lose face and admit huge investment mistakes. As a result, the Japanese financial system became virtually bankrupt while the nation suffered for more than a decade with falling real estate prices during the 1990s and early 2000s. The Japanese economy, which was the world's hyper-growth economy during the previous three decades, went nearly flat during this period, resuming positive growth only in 2004. It can be reasonably argued that the RTC saved the U.S. economy from a similar possible fate.

7. See Bureau of Economic Analysis, National Economic Accounts, "Gross Domestic Product: Percent Change from Preceding Period," http://bea .gov/national/xls/gdpchg.xls.

8. Federal Reserve Board Flow of Funds, www.federalreserve.gov; Commercial Mortgage Securities Association www.cmbs.org; San Francisco Federal Reserve; and National Association of Real Estate Investment Trusts at www.nareit.com. Compiled by RCLCo, Washington, D.C.

9. Christopher B. Leinberger, "The Need for Alternatives to the Nineteen Standard Real Estate Product Types," *Places* 17, no. 2 (July 2005).

10. International Council of Shopping Centers and Urban Land Institute, Dollars and Cents of Shopping Centers, 2006.

11. Tom Wolfe, *A Man in Full* (New York: Farrar, Straus & Giroux, 1998), p. 171.

12. Although many developers, personified by Donald Trump, have the image of being the ultimate gamblers, most are extremely cautious. The name of the game is to minimize all risks up front before any financial exposure is taken, such as, have national credit tenants, use other people's money, do not start a development unless you know your exit strategy, develop only proven conforming products, do not pioneer, have construction-cost guarantees with a bonded construction firm, etc.

13. Robert E. Lang, *Edgeless Cities: Exploring the Elusive Metropolis* (Washington, D.C.: Brookings Institution Press, 2003).

14. U.S. Department of Agriculture, Economic Research Service, "Land Use and Tenure," http://www.ers.usda.gov/; U.S. Census Bureau, Census 1990 and 2000.

CHAPTER 4

1. The tongue-in-cheek phrase "terrestrial affiliation" was coined by George Casey, a residential real estate developer, as he provided the emotional justification for why many homeowners wanted some dirt, no matter how small, to call their own.
2. This is why Manhattan condominiums or co-ops are referred to in a positive manner in advertisements as "prewar." This means to a prospective buyer that a building built prior to the Second World War was of much better construction quality than postwar modern buildings.
3. U.S. Department of Commerce, U.S. Census Bureau, Census 1920 and 2000.
4. Robert Burchell et al., *Sprawl Costs: Economic Impacts of Unchecked Development* (Washington, D.C.: Island Press, 2005).
5. Janna Malamund Smith, *Private Matters: In Defense of the Personal Life* (New York: Addison-Wesley, 1997), 67.
6. Donald C. Shoup, *The High Cost of Free Parking* (Chicago: Planners Press American Planning Association, 2005).
7. U.S. Department of Transportation, Federal Highway Administration, "Highway Statistics 2003," http://www.fhwa.dot.gov/policy/ohim/hs03/htm/hf10.htm.
8. Burchell et al., *Sprawl Costs.*
9. Alan Berube and Bruce Katz, *Katrina's Window: Confronting Concentrated Poverty Across America* (Washington, D.C.: The Brookings Institution, October 2005).
10. U.S. Department of Transportation's Federal Highway Administration, "Highway Statistics 2004," http://www.fhwa.dot.gov/policy/ohim/hs04/htm/dl1c.htm.
11. This estimate is probably low because the best statistic about who drives is the number of licensed individuals, and not every holder of a driver's license has access to a car.
12. Christopher Lasch, *The Revolt of the Elites: and the Betrayal of Democracy,* (New York: W.W. Norton, 1995).

13. Robert D. Putman, *Bowling Alone: The Collapse and Revival of American Community* (New York: Simon & Schuster, 2000).

14. Community Associations Institute, "Industry Data," http://www.caion-line.org/about/facts.cfm.

15. U.S. Department of Agriculture, Economic Research Service, "Data Sets," http://www.ers.usda.gov/Data/; U.S. Census Bureau.

16. The reason for the underreporting of urban land use in recent years is that the U.S. Department of Agriculture uses U.S. Census definitions of urbanized land, which include only residential areas of more than 500 persons per square mile. Using 2.5 persons per household, the U.S. metropolitan average, means that the U.S. Census does not consider land that has two-acre lots as being urbanized. Two-acre lots are often *minimum* densities for McMansions and real mansions, not to mention gentlemen's farms and ranches that are on the exurban fringe of many metropolitan areas, owned by executives that commute into the metropolitan region. None of this kind of residential development would be deemed urbanized by the U.S. Census and hence by the Department of Agriculture. In addition, the U.S. Census reduced metropolitan land area by twenty-one percent after the 1990 Census due to a technical change in their definition, which was a controversial decision.

17. Alan Berube et al., *Finding Exurbia: America's Fast-Growing Communities at the Metropolitan Fringe* (Washington, D.C.: The Brookings Institution, 2006.

18. Ibid.

19. Reid Ewing and John Kostyack, *Endangered by Sprawl: How Runaway Development Threatens America's Wildlife* (Washington, D.C.: National Wildlife Federation, January 2005).

20. Our Built Environment, EPA, January, 2001, 231-R-01-002.

21. Ibid.

22. Ewing and Kostyack, *Endangered by Sprawl.*

23. Bruce A. Stein, Lynn S. Kutner, and Jonathan S. Adams, eds., *Precious Heritage: The Status of Biodiversity in the United States* (New York: Oxford University Press, 2000).

24. U.S. Environmental Protection Agency, Smart Growth Network, "Smart Growth and Urban Heat Islands," http://www.epa.gov/heatisland/resources/pdf/smartgrowthheatislands.pdf.

25. U.S. Environmental Protection Agency, "Protecting Water Resources with Higher-Density Development" (Washington, D.C.: U.S. Environmental Protection Agency, January 2006).

26. Vehicle miles traveled from the U.S. Department of Transportation at www.fhwa.dot.gov and population from U.S. Census at http://www .census.gov/prod/2005pubs/06statab/pop.pdf.

27. Our Built Environment, EPA, January, 2001, 231-R-01-002.

28. R. Ewing and R. Cervero, "Travel and the Built Environment: A Synthesis," *Transportation Research Board Record* no. 1780 (2001): 87–114.

29. Howard Frumkin, Lawrence Frank, and Richard Jackson, *Urban Sprawl and Public Health: Designing, Planning, and Building for Healthy Communities* (Washington, D.C.: Island Press, 2004).

30. Intergovernmental Panel on Climate Change, "Climate Change 2007: The Physical Science Basis," http://www.ipcc.ch/SPM2feb07.pdf.

31. U.S. Environmental Protection Agency, "2007 Draft U.S. Greenhouse Gas Inventory Report," http://epa.gov/climatechange/emissions/usinventory report07.html.

32. Ibid.

33. Lawrence Frank et al., "New Data for a New Era: A Summary of the SMARTRAQ Findings," Smart Growth America, January 2007, http:// www.smartgrowthamerica.org/documents/SMARTRAQSummary_000 .pdf.

34. Dr. William Rees, interview by Dr. Michael Gismondi, 2000, Aurora Online, http://aurora.icaap.org/index.php/aurora/article/view/18/29.

35. Frumkin, Frank, and Jackson, *Urban Sprawl and Public Health*.

36. Lawrence D. Frank, Peter O. Engelke, and Thomas L. Schmid, *Health and Community Design: The Impact of the Built Environment on Physical Activity* (Washington, D.C.: Island Press, 2003).

37. Lawrence Frank and Barbara McCann, "Driving, Walking, and Where You Live: Links to Obesity," http://www.choices4health.org/resource Files/82.pdf.

38. Deborah Cohen et al., *Park Use and Physical Activity in a Sample of Public Parks in the City of Los Angeles* (Arlington, Va.: Rand Corporation, 2006).

39. See Active Living Research, "What We Are Learning," http://www.active livingresearch.org/index.php/What_We_are_Learning/117, for the latest research.

40. Reid H. Ewing, R. Pendall, and D. Chen, "Measuring Sprawl and Its Transportation Impacts," *Transportation Research Record* no. 1828 (2003): 175–183.

41. William H. Lucy and David L. Phillips, *Tomorrow's Cities, Tomorrow's Suburbs* (Chicago: American Planning Association, 2006).

42. Department of Transportation, "Fatality Analysis Reporting System," Bureau of Transportation Statistics http://www.transtats.bts.gov/Data baseInfo.asp?DB_ID=185&DB_Short_Name=FARS&DB_Name=Fat ality%20Analysis%20Reporting%20System%20%28FARS%29&Link =http%3A//www-nrd.nhtsa.dot.gov/departments/nrd-30/ncsa/index .html&DB_URL=.

43. Richard Louv, "Leave No Child Inside," *Orion Magazine,* March/April 2007.

44. U.S. Department of Labor, Bureau of Labor Statistics, "Consumer Expenditure Survey," http://www.bls.gov/cex/.

45. EuroStat Statistical Database of Consumer Expenditure.

46. American Automobile Association, "Your Driving Costs 2006," http:// www.aaapublicaffairs.com/Main/Default.asp?SectionID=&CategoryID= 3&SubCategoryID=9&ContentID=23&.

47. Barbara J. Lipman, "A Heavy Load: The Combined Housing and Transportation Burden of Working Families" (Center for Housing Policy, 2006), http://www.nhc.org/pdf/pub_heavy_load_10_06.pdf.

48. Robert W. Burchell et al., *Sprawl Costs,* 75, 80.

49. Envision Utah, "Envision Utah Quality Control Strategy and Technical Review," January 2000, http://www.envisionutah.org/pdf/January2000 .pdf.

50. These estimates in Utah are made between the reality that is on the ground today, dominated by low-density suburban development in the late 1990s, when the planning was undertaken, and only a slightly higher average density over the next ten to twenty years, which would still be predominantly drivable sub-urbanism, because it has to include everything on the ground. It vastly understates the *marginal* cost differences between drivable sub-urbanism and walkable urbanism. It does not compare one more unit of low-density suburban development, say a house at one unit to the acre, versus one more unit of high-density walkable urbanism, say a condominium unit at forty units to the acre—forty times as dense as standard suburban development.

51. James Duncan and Associates, *The Search for Efficient Urban Growth Patterns: A Study of the Fiscal Impacts of Development in Florida* (Report presented to the Governor's Task Force on Urban Growth and the Florida Department of Community Affairs, Florida, July 1989), 13.

52. Go to http://www.cabq.gov/council/impactfees.html for information about the City of Albuquerque impact fee system, which passed in 2003. The author served on the impact fee advisory panel, and the studies backing up the impact fee legislation justified fees that were twice as high as those implemented.

53. American Society of Civil Engineers, "Report Card for America's Infrastructure," http://www.asce.org/reportcard/2005/.

54. Congressional Research Service, Report for Congress, "Energy: Selected Facts and Numbers," November 29, 2006, http://ncseonline.org/NLE/CRSreports/06Dec/RL31849.pdf.

55. Testimony of Congressman Roscoe Bartlett before Congress on February 8, 2006, http://www.peakoil.net/Publications/PeakOilSpclOrder%2315TextCharts020806Low.pdf. House Committee on Energy and Commerce, Subcommittee on Energy and Air Quality, "Understanding the Peak Oil Theory," 109th Cong., 1st sess., 2005, http://www.access.gpo.gov/congress/index.html.

56. Robert L. Hirsch, Roger Bezdek, and Robert Wendling, "Peaking of World Oil Production: Impacts, Mitigation, and Risk Management," *321Energy,* March, 2005, http://www.321energy.com/editorials/hirsch/hirsch031705.html.

57. "Survey of the World Economy," *The Economist,* September 14, 2006, http://www.economist.com/surveys/displayStory.cfm?story_id=7877959.

58. James Howard Kunstler, *The Long Emergency: Surviving the Converging Catastrophes of the Twenty-First Century* (New York: Atlantic Monthly Press, 2005).

59. Hirsch, Bezdek, and Wendling, "Peaking of World Oil Production."

60. Thomas Friedman, "Addicted to Oil," *The New York Times,* February 1, 2006.

61. Michael D'Arcy, Michael O'Hanlon, et al. *Protecting the Homeland* (Washington, D.C.: The Brookings Institution Press, 2006).

62. This is a calculation by the author assuming that sixty percent of gasoline prices are a result of the cost of crude oil; the rest is for processing and distribution.

CHAPTER 5

1. Arthur C. Nelson, "Leadership in a New Era/Comment on 'Planning Leadership in a New Era,'" *Journal of the American Planning Association,* (Autumn 2006): 393.

2. Dowell Myers et al., "The Coming Demand" (Congress for the New Urbanism, October 9, 2001), http://www.cnu.org/sites/files/Coming_Demand .pdf.

3. Ibid.

4. "Battle for Brainpower," *The Economist,* October 7, 2006, U.S. ed.

5. Anton C. Nelessen, *Visions for a New American Dream: Process, Principles, and an Ordinance to Plan and Design Small Communities,* 2nd ed. (Chicago: American Planning Association, 1994), 88.

6. Jonathan Levine, Aseem Inam, and Gwo-Wei Torng, "A Choice-Based Rationale for Land-Use and Transportation Alternatives: Evidence from Boston and Atlanta," *Journal of Planning Education and Research* 24, no. 3 (2005): 317–330.

7. Jonathan Levine and Lawrence D. Frank, "Transportation and Land Use Preferences and Residents' Neighborhood Choices: The Sufficiency of Compact Development in the Atlanta Region," *Transportation* 34, no. 2 (March 2007): 255–274.

8. Lawrence Frank et al., "New Data for a New Era: A Summary of the SMARTRAQ Findings" (Smart Growth America, January 2007), http:// www.smartgrowthamerica.org/documents/SMARTRAQSummary_000 .pdf.

9. Belden, Russonello, and Stewart, Smart Growth America, "2004 National Community Preference Survey," (October 2004), http://www.smart growthamerica.org/documents/NAR-SGASurvey.pdf.

10. The comparative research for these metropolitan areas was gathered from http://www.realtor.com.

11. Ibid.

12. National Association of Realtors, http://www.realtor.org/research/index. html.

13. *New York Times,* "Small but Sufficient," January 19, 2007, Late edition-final.

14. Housing prices are notoriously "sticky," meaning that sellers tend not to discount list prices, though many hidden discounts are offered (e.g.,

sellers paying closing costs, upgrades being included at no cost, or even individual houses being taken off the market to await a better market). As a result, the sales pace can be a better indicator of market strength or weakness than sales price.

15. Brian Louis, "Toll Calls Spring 'A Bust,' Can't Predict Recovery," Bloomberg.com, March 15, 2007, http://www.bloomberg.com/apps/news?pid=2 0601087&sid=aVnXzDLdZ5fA&refer=home (accessed March 15, 2007).

16. Internal RCLCo research performed for this book.

17. Tysons Corner in 2007 is accessible only by car and rather poor bus service. However, the Metro rail system will serve the area by 2012. Hopes are that the coming of the Metro will convert this sprawling drivable sub-urban place into a walkable urban location, which will be a daunting task given the huge eight-lane streets that bisect it.

18. Internal Brookings Institution research performed for this book.

19. Land does not make anything, except when it is used for agricultural crops. Agricultural land prices are far below those for urbanized land, ranging from $500 to 20,000 per acre. Translating that into square foot prices gives only a penny a square foot for agricultural land at the low end to forty-seven cents a square foot at the high end. Almost any urbanized land use, such as housing or commercial, will start at $20,000 per acre (forty-seven cents per square foot) and go up dramatically from there. This value jump from agricultural land to urbanized land explains why many farmers are eager to see sprawl take subdivisions to an ever expanding metropolitan fringe.

20. State of the Cities Data System (SOCDS) Building Permits Database, http://socds.huduser.org/permits/.

21. www.census.gov/const/C30/totsa.pdf. May 2007.

22. Internal Brookings Institution research performed for this book.

23. Nelson, "Longer View."

24. Internal Brookings Institution research performed for this book.

25. Michael Corkery, "Mr. Toll Turns to Towers," *Wall Street Journal,* December 13, 2006.

26. Jonathan D. Miller, *Emerging Trends in Real Estate 2006* (Washington, D.C.: Urban Land Institute, 2006).

27. Bre Edmonds, "Transit-Oriented Development Sweeps Suburbia," *Real Estate Business Online,* February 26, 2007, http://www.rebusinessonline .com/article_archive/02-26-07.shtml.

CHAPTER 6

1. There are other popular measures of density, for example "dwelling units per acre" or "persons per acre." These two measures are appropriate only for residential uses, not commercial or industrial uses. FAR can be used for all types of real estate uses.

2. There is "gross" FAR and "net" FAR. This book is using gross FAR. Gross FAR includes all of the land used for transportation circulation (streets, sidewalks, transit lines, parks, stand-alone parking lots and decks, etc.) as well as the buildings and the parking lot or decks connected with the building. Net FAR includes only the buildings and the land under the parking lot or decks connected to the building in its calculation. Gross FAR will be a lower number than net FAR when measuring a particular building because the denominator (land) is larger than in the calculation for net FAR while the building square footage is the same. Gross FAR can be applied to a district because it includes the common area used for transportation and parks surrounding various buildings.

3. Readers familiar with the New Urbanism concept, the Transect, will note a slight difference with the two broad types of development referred to in this book. The Transect makes the point that the built environment runs smoothly on a continuum from low to high density; there are no breaks along that continuum. This book postulates that there is a break in density on the Transect between T-3 (suburban) and T-4 (general urban). The promises of drivable sub-urbanism can best be achieved at very low densities of less than 0.3 FAR. Walkable urbanism needs to have four to five times the density of drivable sub-urbanism to achieve the character it promises. The Transect is an extremely useful construct, but it is not as smooth as some graphic depictions of it might suggest.

4. Concentrated poverty, discussed in chapter 4, is generally considered the primary culprit in the failure of high rise public housing built following Le Corbusier. The public housing schemes that replaced these troubled high-rise projects in the 1990s are almost all mixed-use, mixed-income walkable urbanism. This approach was pioneered during the Clinton administration under the direction of Henry Cisneros, secretary of housing and urban development. Following the New Urbanism planning approach, many of these Hope VI housing projects were built with sixty percent market-rate housing and forty percent affordable housing in a

low-rise but high-density plan. As of 2006, these projects have proven to be quite successful in reducing crime and integrating families with different incomes, although management is the key to this experiment, so only time will tell if this is a long-term solution. The Bush administration significantly reduced funding for the Hope VI program.

5. A version of Le Corbusier's Plan Voisin is still rising in many European suburbs. Most Americans' image of European cities is the (still-standing) Left Bank, Las Rambles in Barcelona, and the West End of London, all magical walkable urban places. However, much new European suburban development is neverland, drivable density. This kind of suburban development was infamously seen in the media during the race riots in France's suburbs in 2005.

6. Parking ratios are used to measure the amount of parking required by each use. Parking ratios are based upon the number of parking spaces for 1,000 square feet of building. For a drivable neighborhood-serving retail center, anchored by a grocery store, the ratio is approximately five to six parking spaces per 1,000 square feet, or 1,500–2,100 square feet of parking for every 1,000 square feet of store. For a restaurant or movie theater, you need between eight and ten parking spaces per 1,000 square feet of building or 2,400–3,500 square feet of parking for every 1,000 square feet of building. Conventional apartment buildings need 2.5 parking spaces per unit, or a parking ratio of about two spaces for every 1,000 square feet. However, Donald Shoup, author of the *High Price of Free Parking*, contended that none of these parking ratios are based on any scientific inquiry about actual parking needs, and are almost universally inflated, working under the assumption that you can never have too much parking. Donald C. Shoup, *The High Cost of Free Parking* (Chicago: Planners Press American Planning Association, 2005).

7. For the sake of disclosure, the author's development company develops New Urbanist neighborhoods. In addition, one of my partners in that company is the developer of Seaside. Finally, a corporate development partner of my company is the developer of Stapleton in Denver.

8. Downtown Washington, D.C., was a "basket case" in the 1980s and 1990s, following the riots of the 1960s and the suburban flight of the 1970s and 1980s also experienced elsewhere. Downtown D.C. continually lost office space market share for the sixty-five years from 1940 to 2005. Virtually 100 percent of the region's office space was in downtown

in 1940; the rate fell until it reached its trough of thirty-three percent in 2004. Virtually nobody lived in downtown, and all but one department store had left. Then it all changed. Following an aggressively managed private-sector-led revitalization, first of urban entertainment, then rental housing, and then for-sale residential, the downtown has been revitalizing faster than probably any downtown in the country. Then the office market took off, and in 2005 Washington absorbed forty percent of the office space that year, and in 2006 it absorbed forty-six percent of the office space that year. By the mid-2000s, downtown office vacancy was a very low seven percent and rental rates were sixty percent above the suburbs (from RCLCo private research based upon CoStar data).

Downtown San Diego, which in the 1980s was where sailors went to get drunk and prostitutes shared the sidewalks with the homeless, has seen seventy new housing projects each year during the early part of the 2000s. The arrival of the new Padres baseball stadium, which opened in 2005, pushed the boundaries of downtown eight blocks farther to the east. The downtown population was a very respectable 17,000 in 2000, and it doubled to 35,000 by 2005.

9. The most complex and dense downtown in the country is, of course, Midtown Manhattan. Midtown is filled with hundreds of thousands of rental apartments and for-sale townhouses and flats, millions of square feet of retail and restaurants, the largest concentration of office space in the country, and tens of thousands of hotel rooms. It is the home of a large government office concentration—the United Nations. Then there are the museums, art galleries, Broadway theaters, the jewelry district, business and social clubs, and the southern part of Central Park, with its zoo and ice-staking rink. There are grocery stores, sidewalk merchants, and horse-drawn carriages. There are art, ethnic, and athletic events every weekend, as well as political and social protests about issues from gay marriage to abortion. More people (82%) walk or take transit to work in Manhattan than any other place in the country, ten times greater than the country as a whole. The FAR of Midtown Manhattan is probably approaching 30.0, and the rich complexity is beyond any other place in the country.

10. Pasadena, like many suburban towns, was once connected to the larger region by a transit system that was infamously torn out in the 1960s. The new light rail system serving Pasadena opened in 2005.

11. The other well-known east coast "new town" was Columbia, Maryland, developed by Jim Rouse. It too was a drivable sub-urban place with walking trails leading nowhere practical. It did include a unique affordable housing, mixed-race focus, a legacy of Rouse and his wife, Patty. Only in the mid-2000s was the regional mall, the center of Columbia, undergoing planning to be retrofitted as a walkable urban place.

12. Randall Shearin, "Mastering Mixed-Use," *Shopping Center Business,* June 2007, 58.

13. Number is based upon the unpublished research of Arthur C. Nelson, which combines base data from National Research/CoStar, the International Council of Shopping Centers, and the information on the Web site www.deadmalls.com (amazing the things people follow). The definition of "dead and dying mall" is from www.deadmalls.com: "A mall with a high vacancy rate, low consumer traffic level, or is [sic] dated and deteriorating in some manner." This estimate includes regional malls, power centers, and neighborhood-serving malls.

14. Rosslyn, Virginia, got a decidedly bad start as the first of these walkable urban places. It is a poor compromise between being walkable and car-friendly, much to the detriment of the public realm. County leaders recognize this, as does everyone else, and know that a retrofit is required to make it a more attractive walkable urban place, as are the rest of the Metro station-anchored places in Arlington County.

15. American Podiatric Medical Association, "An American Podiatric Medical Association Study Reveals Top Ten Walker-Friendly Cities," http://www.apma.org/s_apma/doc.asp?CID=24&DID=17913.

16. Over the years, university and college presidents have seen their job descriptions change radically. Initially they were academics who had an administrative flair; they then evolved into being nearly full-time fund raisers. Many university and college presidents have recently become real estate developers, following the lead of Judith Rodin when she was president of the University of Pennsylvania in the 1990s and her then chief real estate staff person, John Fry, who is now president of Franklin & Marshall College in Lancaster, Pennsylvania.

17. Arthur C. Nelson, "Longer View: Leadership in a New Era," *Journal of the American Planning Association,* (Autumn 2006).

18. Office of the Chief Financial Officer, District of Columbia. Citizens Financial Report 2006. http://cfo.dc.gov/cfo/frames.asp?doc=/cfo/lib/cfo/

cafr/2006/citizens_financial_report_2006.pdf and previous years on the same Web site.

19. See the Center City Academic Region Web site at http://www.center citycschools.com.

20. A good reference for changing the perspective of neighborhood groups is *Choosing Our Community's Future: A Citizens Guide to Getting the Most Out of New Development,* by David Goldberg at Smart Growth America. http://sgusa.convio.net/site/PageServer?pagename=guidebook.

21. "Block level" refers to a walkable street that connects the two sides of that street; the street is a connector, not a divider. Each block is the two sides of a unifying street. The boundaries of the block are the property lines to the rear, many times demarcated by an alley. Streets in drivable sub-urban commercial districts tend to be dividers, particularly for pedestrians.

22. There are many good and not-so-good reasons to discount the Washington, D.C., area as a potential model for the country's future. Much can be learned from the Washington area about how to take advantage of the existing pent-up demand for walkable urbanism. The city contains an example of each of the five types of regional-serving walkable urban places; no other metro area has an example of all five. Even if the lessons are to be applied to a metro area that does not house the national government (a good reason to discount Washington as a potential model), D.C. has had the national government for 200 years. The walkable urban transformation described in this book took place over just the past ten to fifteen years; before and after the changes the national government has been in D.C.

23. RCLCo private research based upon CoStar data of the Washington, D.C., region office market, 1985–2007.

24. Downtown, Midtown, Royal Oak, and Birmingham.

CHAPTER 7

1. Atlanta Housing Authority, "AHA Quick Facts," http://www.atlanta housingauth.org/pressroom/index.cfm?Fuseaction=quickfacts.

2. Montgomery County Planning.org, "Affordable Housing in Montgomery County," http://www.mc-mncppc.org/research/analysis/housing/affordable/housing_toc.shtm#trends.

3. See Danielle Arigoni, "Affordable Housing and Smart Growth: Making the Connection" (Washington, D.C.: National Neighborhood Association, 2001), http://www.epa.gov/dced/pdf/epa_ah_sg.pdf.
4. Council on Affordable Housing, "COAH's Third Round Handbook," 2nd ed. (August 2006), http://www.state.nj.us/dca/coah/round3resources.shtml.
5. The residents of the walkable urban area around the Silver Spring, Maryland Metro station, just over the District of Columbia border, are very concerned about the decline in affordable housing over recent years. Ironically, the single family neighborhood surrounding this high-density place recently defeated a proposal to allow granny flats, fearing that the dreaded "others" would invade their sanctuary.
6. For more information, see Christopher B. Leinberger, "Taming Gentrification: Using Rising Values to Finance Affordable Housing Through 'Value Latching,'" http://www.cleinberger.com/AdminHome.asp?ArticleID=205.
7. Arthur C. Nelson, "Leadership in a New Era/Comment on 'Planning Leadership in a New Era,'" *Journal of the American Planning Association,* (Autumn 2006).
8. Alan Berube et al., *Finding Exurbia: America's Fast-Growing Communities at the Metropolitan Fringe* (Washington, D.C.: The Brookings Institution, 2006.
9. U.S. Department of Agriculture, "Farmers Market Facts," http://www.ams.usda.gov/farmersmarkets/facts.htm.

CHAPTER 8

1. Based upon the size of a king's foot, the weight of silver as a currency in the fourteenth century, and other arbitrary accidents of history, the English measurement system is absolutely irrational. But it has proven to be too difficult to drop in favor of the current world standard, the metric system. Congress passed the Metric Conversion Act in 1975, and President Ford signed it into law. It established the United States Metric Board in 1976, but it was dissolved by 1982. The proposed conversion was a complete failure, so the United States is joined by only two other countries out of the 190 countries on the planet in not officially using the metric system.
2. Euclidean zoning is named after a major Supreme Court ruling in 1926, based upon a case from Euclid, Ohio, which upheld the legality of zoning

that mandated separation of uses from one another. The phrase "Euclidean zoning" has such a high-brow sound to it, yet it has nothing to do with the ancient Greek mathematician.

3. City of Albuquerque, *The Downtown 2010 Sector Development Plan,* (2000), http://www.cabq.gov/planning/publications.

4. Annie Gowen, "County Board Approves Plan for a Quicker, Quirkier Claredon," *The Washington Post,* December 10, 2006.

5. Arthur C. Nelson, "Leadership in a New Era/Comment on 'Planning Leadership in a New Era,'" *Journal of the American Planning Association,* (Autumn 2006).

6. City of Albuquerque, "2005 Regulatory Plan: Hunning-Highland EDo Urban Conservation Overlay Zone (UCOZ)," (March 2005), http://www.cabq.gov/planning/publications/pdf/EDo.pdf.

7. A popular technique for creating such streets is the "road diet," which reduces the number of lanes by adding parking on the sides, often adds a turn lane, and increases traffic flow.

8. There are two elements of finance: equity and debt. Debt includes loans, mortgages, or bonds that are first in line to be repaid by a project or company. Debt involves the least risk due to this first position and thus charge the lowest relative interest for the money invested. Equity is cash, land, an existing building or professional fees invested that will be paid off after debt is serviced on an annual basis and is therefore at much greater risk. As a result, equity has much higher return expectations than debt. In conventionally financed real estate development, equity is about twenty percent of the total money invested in the project and debt is about eighty percent.

9. For more in-depth discussion of patient equity and financing walkable urbanism, see The Brookings Institution Metropolitan Policy Program, "Back to the Future: The Need for Patient Equity in Real Estate Finance," (January 2007), http://www.brookings.edu/metro/walkable_urbanism.htm.

10. Stephen Ross, speech, 20th UM/ULI Real Estate Forum, Detroit, MI, October 27, 2006.

11. Office of the Governor, "Gov. Blagojevich Signs New Law to Expand Affordable Housing Options for Illinois Working Families," *Illinois Government News Network,* June 30, 2006, http://www.illinois.gov/Press Releases/ShowPressRelease.cfm?SubjectID=2&RecNum=5034 (accessed

Feb. 2007); Good Jobs First, "Linking Jobs to Transit, Housing," April 14, 2006, http://www.goodjobsfirst.org/news/article.cfm?id=117 (accessed Feb. 2007).

12. American Association of State Highway and Transportation Officials, "President Bush Signs Transportation Reauthorization Bill," August 10, 2005, http://transportation1.org/aashtonew/?sid=278; American Association of State Highway and Transportation Officials, "Transit Advocates Praise Signing," August 10, 2005, http://transportation1.org/aashtonew/?sid=281.

13. Allocations to the following programs: Interstate, Bridge, National Highway System, Surface Transportation Program, and Highway Safety Improvement Program, Minimum Guarantee, Equity Bonus.

14. Robert Puentes and Linda Bailey, *Improving Metropolitan Decision Making in Transportation: Greater Funding and Devolution for Greater Accountability* (Washington, D.C.: Brookings Institution, 2003).

15. Many state legislatures are still disproportionately controlled by rural interests, not the fast-growing metropolitan areas. The seniority system and out-of-date legislative jurisdictions keep road building at the top of the transportation agenda in most states.

16. Puentes and Bailey, *Improving Metropolitan Decision Making in Transportation*.

17. Surface Transportation Policy Partnership, "Ten Years of Progress: Building Better Communities Through Transportation," (Washington, D.C.: STTP, January 1, 2002), http://www.transact.org/report.asp?id=59.

18. America Bikes, "Billions for Bikes: The Potential in SAFETEA-LU," http://www.americabikes.org.

19. New Jersey Department of Transportation, "New Jersey FIT: Future in Transportation," http://www.nj.gov/transportation/works/njfit/.

20. The New Jersey DOT is the first to embrace smart growth as a direct solution to its mission to provide mobility to state residents. The state DOT, tired of building more and more lanes to keep up with development, is now actively working with communities to plan the road network and place developments in ways that do not promote more traffic growth. The NJDOT offers planning funds to local communities that agree to work with the agency on master plans for major road corridors—and declines to invest in areas that refuse to rein in sprawling development. The agency's staff, trained by some of the leading smart growth consultants

in the country, present growth scenarios that clarify the dysfunctions of sprawling development and conduct innovative planning studies. Projects undertaken have included the scrapping of highway bypasses and widenings in favor of helping construct a new local street grid with in-fill development. One study found that ninety-three percent of existing traffic would be better served by local road improvements than by the long-planned bypass. In downtown Newark a boulevard is being redesigned to encourage pedestrian travel instead of adding traffic lanes. Although New Jersey is a home-rule state, the collaborative and funded planning process fosters local buy-in. The NJDOT is also actively promoting transit with its Transit Village program, which offers technical assistance plus capital for transit-oriented developments. Watch this video to see how this can be discussed in a way that is attractive to communities: http://www.nj.gov/transportation/works/njfit/video.shtm.

21. The political agency for managing the metropolitan transportation infrastructure already exists; it is the metropolitan planning organization (MPO). Every metropolitan area in the country has an MPO and by bypassing the state DOTs and directly funding the MPOs for the transportation needs of their region, there would be a chance of more walkable urban transportation systems being created. Like everything else in politics, this is easier said than done. State DOTs are among the most powerful agencies in the state government, and many governors are more beholden to the DOT director than vice versa.

22. The Regional Transportation District, http://www.rtd-denver.com.

23. Center for Transportation Excellence, "Transportation Finance at the Ballot Box: Voters Support Increased Investment and Choice," (2006), http://www.cfte.org/CFTE%20Election%20Trends%20Report.pdf.

24. David Feehan and Marvin Feit, *Making Business Districts,* (New York: The Haworth Press, 2006), p. 62.

25. Achieving critical mass is the goal of all redeveloping and developing walkable urban places. The definition of critical mass is not overly scientific; it is like pornography—you know it when you see it.

26. Internal Brookings research performed for this book.

27. Dr. James E. Hansen, "A Conversation with Dr. James Hansen: Global Warming Controversy," interview by Andrew C. Revkin, *New York Times,* http://video.on.nytimes.com/?fr_story=cd3d476b15fec65dc1f1ee82cb619 4d532c96858.

28. U.S. Bureau of the Census
29. As David Owen wrote in *The New Yorker:* "By the most significant measures, New York [City] is the greenest community in the country and one of the greenest in the world. [If] New York City was granted statehood, it would rank 51st in percentage of energy usage." *The New Yorker,* October 18, 2004.

Index

f indicates entries in figures, n indicates endnote numbers.

ABOUT ISLAND PRESS

Island Press is the only nonprofit organization in the United States whose principal purpose is the publication of books on environmental issues and natural resource management. We provide solutions-oriented information to professionals, public officials, business and community leaders, and concerned citizens who are shaping responses to environmental problems.

Since 1984, Island Press has been the leading provider of timely and practical books that take a multidisciplinary approach to critical environmental concerns. Our growing list of titles reflects our commitment to bringing the best of an expanding body of literature to the environmental community throughout North America and the world.

Support for Island Press is provided by the Agua Fund, The Geraldine R. Dodge Foundation, Doris Duke Charitable Foundation, The Ford Foundation, The William and Flora Hewlett Foundation, The Joyce Foundation, Kendeda Sustainability Fund of the Tides Foundation, The Forrest & Frances Lattner Foundation, The Henry Luce Foundation, The John D. and Catherine T. MacArthur Foundation, The Marisla Foundation, The Andrew W. Mellon Foundation, Gordon and Betty Moore Foundation, The Curtis and Edith Munson Foundation, Oak Foundation, The Overbrook Foundation, The David and Lucile Packard Foundation, Wallace Global Fund, The Winslow Foundation, and other generous donors.

The opinions expressed in this book are those of the author(s) and do not necessarily reflect the views of these foundations.